ORTRUD GRIEB

COMPANION PLANTING

CREATE A FLOURISHING KITCHEN GARDEN
BY MATCHMAKING YOUR PLANTS

GREEN BOOKS
LONDON • OXFORD • NEW YORK • NEW DELHI • SYDNEY

CONTENTS

- **4** **Companion planting basics**
- 6 What is companion planting?
- 10 Advantages of companion planting
- 16 In practice
- 17 A mini mulch ABC
- 18 Typical jobs for spring
- 19 Typical jobs for autumn
- **20** **Template beds for beginners**
- 22 Ten tried and tested beginner beds throughout the year
- 24 Celeriac–leek–broccoli bed
- 26 Lettuce–beans–brassica bed
- 28 Tomato–cabbage bed
- 30 Cucumber–beetroot–onion bed
- 32 Carrot–sugarsnap pea bed
- 34 Courgette–sweetcorn bed
- 36 Potato–broad bean–strawberry bed
- 38 Strawberry–garlic–French marigold bed
- 40 Strawberry–garlic bed
- 42 Strawberry–green manure bed
- 43 Plant families
- 44 Mixed-row cultivation with clover paths

52	Companion plants in containers	70	Yacon bed
54	Raised beds for plentiful fresh vegetables	72	Potato bed as recommended by Margarete Langerhorst
56	Good neighbours under the tomato roof	74	Shallot–carrot–black salsify–chicory bed
		76	Celery–cauliflower–leek–parsnip bed
58	**Model beds for the adventurous**	78	Baby beet–kohl rabi–bean bed
60	A constant supply of fresh salad	80	Colourful tomato bed
62	Green manure for pre- or post-sowing	82	Mixed-row cultivation for the adventurous
64	Eight sample beds for the adventurous	84	Colourful row plan
66	Native American bed	**88**	**Helpful planning tips**
68	Pea–carrot–brassica–horseradish bed	92	**Index**
		95	**Photo credits**

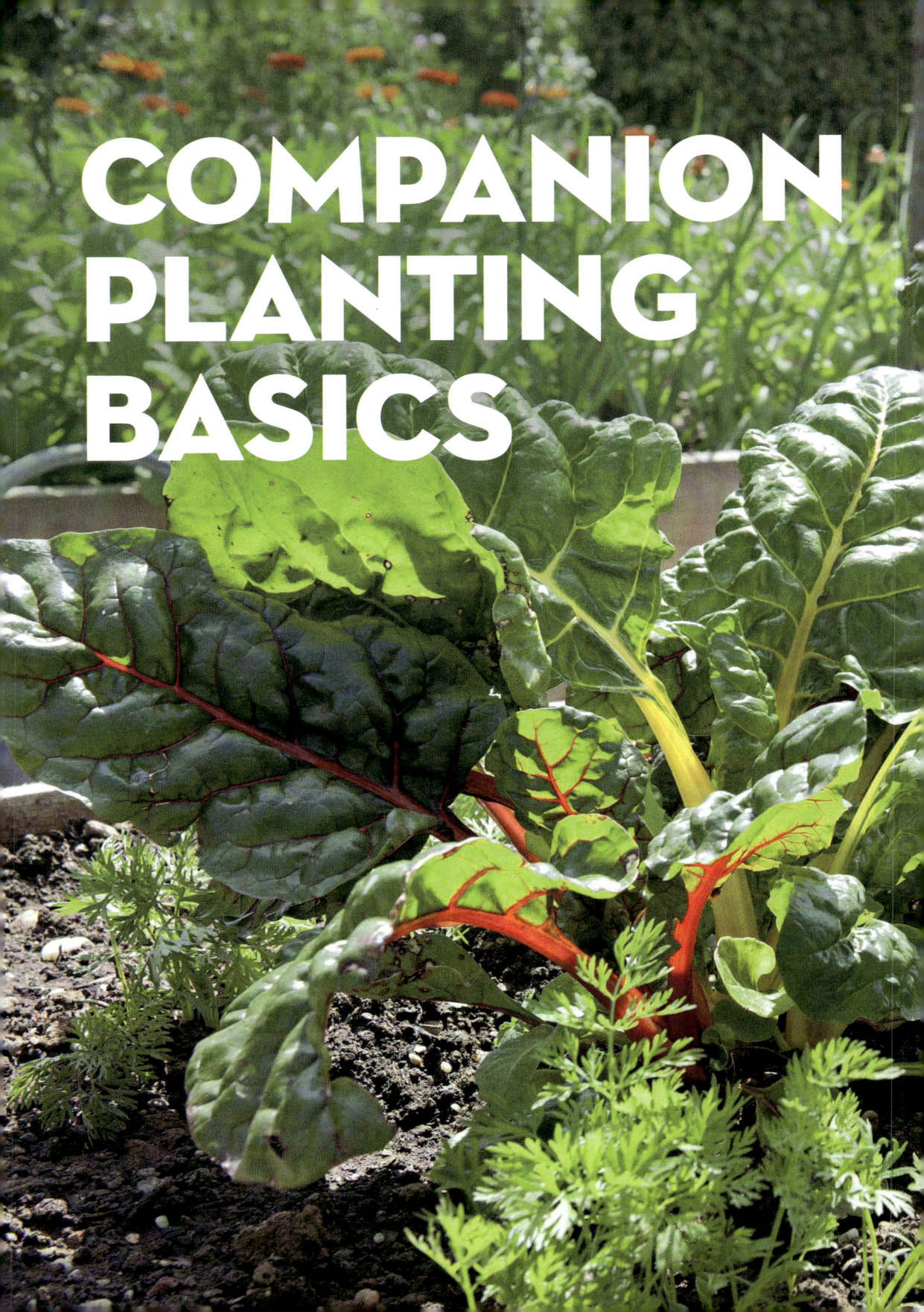

COMPANION PLANTING BASICS

What is companion planting?

Companion planting is no longer only used by idealistic organic gardeners. Research from across the world proves that consciously selecting neighbours for plants impacts how they grow.

Anyone who walks into a vegetable garden that has adopted companion planting will be greeted by a kaleidoscope of colours. Under tomato plants, nasturtiums grow among parsley. Green runner beans wind around sweetcorn (maize) plants, with bright orange squashes flourishing underneath. Among the cucumbers are fragrant basil and dill flowers, and rows of vibrant, red-stemmed beetroot. Meanwhile bees buzz, hoverflies hover and butterflies flutter over this little paradise.

BETTER GROWTH WITH COMPANIONS

Companion planting allows a medley of different plants to grow together, mutually benefiting each other by deterring pests or boosting soil and plant health. In order to achieve this, the soil should be kept fertile by surface mulching. In scientific trials, good partnerships between plants have produced higher yields and reduced the effects of disease. Although gardeners have been monitoring companion planting of vegetables in their gardens for decades, they have not always agreed in their observations. This is not surprising, as the influence of plants on each other is heavily dependent on other factors, such as the number and types of soil organisms present.

THE MAGIC OF PLANTS

In nature, many plant species seem to grow happily next to each other. However, despite this apparently peaceful coexistence there is often well-concealed but fierce competition. Above ground, plants compete for sunlight by adjusting the positioning of their leaves toward the sun, with the uppermost leaves gaining the greatest advantage. Meanwhile, below ground the roots compete for nutrients and water. On top of this, plants use biochemical tactics to release compounds via the leaves and roots, which are also present in decaying plant material. When these compounds are processed by the organisms in the soil, some of them will be converted to highly toxic substances that damage neighbouring plants, sometimes even killing them. For example, it has been shown that wheat secretes compounds that prevents lettuce seeds from germinating and inhibits root growth. In fact, wheat is even better at suppressing lettuce than chemical herbicides. Meanwhile, rice only produces growth-suppressing compounds if genetically different plants are growing nearby. Although the production of such compounds means it grow more slowly, it is also more resistant to pests and diseases.

1. Gardens with companion planting have a heavenly array of colours and shapes.

2. Vertically growing palm kale and sprawling ground-covering nasturtiums form a dream pairing – and not just visually.

GROWTH THROUGH LOVE

In scientific trials, sweetcorn and beans grown together produced a higher total yield than when each was planted as a single crop. Strawberries planted with onions, or celeriac planted with leeks, were also highly successful pairings. When infested with pests, many plants 'warn' each other of these attacks by releasing volatile scented compounds so that the neighbouring plants can arm themselves chemically. Particular odours are also used to attract predators of pests, to prevent fungal spores from germinating, or to confuse the pests' sense of smell. Since the concept of companion planting was first developed, there have been lengthy debates about the mechanisms involved in its success. However, there is no question that it delivers far healthier vegetables in times of need.

Thousands of years ago, Native Americans developed what is now the most well-known companion-planting system to maintain the fertility of their soils, known as the 'Three Sisters'. This method involves growing sweetcorn, beans and squash together because these crops support each other. In fact, sweetcorn and beans could potentially solve the problems caused by intensive cultivation of sweetcorn as a single crop.

Worldwide use of intercropping

In China, India and many tropical countries around the world, farmers have long practiced intercropping – growing two or more crops in the same area. In regions where many people rely on limited land for food, intercropping increases yields by making more efficient use of space and resources.

The 'Three Sisters' growing together in a plot that has embraced the concept of companion planting.

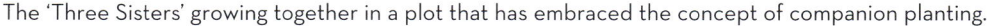

Effects of allelopathy and monocultures

Records dating back to 300 BC evidence our interest in positive and negative relationships between plants. An early example of this is the black walnut tree (*Juglans nigra*) which has long been known to harm neighbouring plants. We now know that walnut trees secrete a chemical compound called juglone into the soil, which inhibits the growth of many plants in the vicinity, but particularly tomatoes and apples. In 1937 the term 'allelopathy' was coined to describe this kind of harmful chemical interaction between plants.

> Around 1800, declining agricultural yields were increasingly attributed to monoculture, and by 1830, the term 'soil fatigue' was coined in England to describe this effect.

The history of companion planting

During the Second World War, in a movement spearheaded by resourceful women, a range of different vegetable crops were grown together in the same space to maximise production at a time of severe food shortages. Cultivation had to be labour- and time-efficient. In Germany, from 1935 onwards, Gertrud Franck supplied her family and servants with vegetables grown on her large farm. To do this, she developed her renowned energy-saving system of mixed-row cultivation. Newspaper articles, lectures and her book, *Companion Planting: Successful Gardening the Organic Way* (1983), led to an explosion of interest in companion planting in the 1980s. In 1983 I had the privilege of learning about companion planting from Jakobus and Margarete Langerhorst in their gigantic vegetable garden in Austria. At the time, Jakobus was poring over his garden plans and notes every evening in order to optimise his companion planting. His book was then published in 1986, and Margarete's in 1996. I am very grateful to them both for their input, as it has played a big part in my becoming self-sufficient in vegetables for over 40 years now.

Blue-podded pea using sweetcorn as a climbing support. Beneath, squashes keep the ground shaded.

Advantages of companion planting

A garden that has adopted companion planting is colourful and beautiful, it provides habitat for a wide range of wildlife, and there is always something to harvest somewhere – but that is not all.

In 2020, Dutch and Chinese scientists calculated in a metastudy of 500 data sets that in mixed cultivation typically a third less fertiliser was required. On average, harvest yields from European fields were 16 per cent higher, and in China they were 30 per cent higher, than when only one type of plant was growing in a field. Many trials involved mixtures of legumes and cereals, which have now been thoroughly researched, but there are also obvious advantages to using mixed-cultivation vegetable beds in other parts of Europe.

MORE FERTILE SOIL

In companion planting, the ground is almost completely covered with plants, mulch and crop residues. This ground cover prevents the surface soil from being eroded by strong wind, washed away by heavy rains or compacted by treading. Furthermore, the soil does not dry out so easily as it is buffered from extremes of temperature. This is hugely beneficial for the soil organisms that decompose the mulch, which means they will release even more valuable nutrients. Similarly, microorganisms will produce more humus – a rich organic matter formed by decomposing insects, plants and leaves. Importantly, these soil organisms improve the structure of the soil so that it develops a loose, crumbly texture and retains moisture much more effectively. While it is best not to tread on soil, as this can compromise its structure, fertile soil will feel

Earthworms improve the soil structure and make it fertile.

With ground cover provided by mulch and plants, soil organisms will thrive.

slightly springy when walked on. It is not necessary to dig over your soil at all, and this will save you from a lot of tiring work and allows the soil organisms to happily work away undisturbed. The activity of those organisms releases plenty of nutrients for our vegetables, reducing the need for fertilisers. Above all, this soil type is easy to work with and remains fertile over a long period.

OPTIMUM NUTRIENT UTILISATION

Shallow-rooted plants such as radishes only put roots down in the top 20cm of the soil. In the event of heavy rainfall the nutrients at this depth will be leached downwards through the soil and will no longer be available to these plants. In companion planting, for every shallow-rooting crop, such as radishes or lettuces, the aim is to have a deep-rooting crop, such as tomato plants. The latter will take up nutrients and water from deep down in the soil (from depths of up to 2m in extreme cases). When the remains of the tomato plants decompose after harvesting, they will release nutrients into the surface layers of the soil.

How to identify a fertile soil

Fertile soil is dark, with a loose, crumbly texture, and it smells good. When it rains heavily the soil structure remains stable, and so long as it is not walked on it will not become compacted. When the soil is damp and its temperature is around 10–15°C you will often see particularly large numbers of earthworms. On fertile soils you will find that not only vegetables but also weeds such as nettles, chickweed and gallant soldier grow really well!

1. Where no vegetables are growing, sow phacelia. This attracts bees all summer long and is killed off by frost in the winter.

2. Nitrogen-collecting legumes can be identified by their butterfly-like flowers.

3. Shallow- and deep-rooting plants, and those with high and low demands for nutrients, planted together and completely covering the ground.

4. Nitrogen deficient cape gooseberries. The lower leaves are turning yellow.

Different vegetables vary in their rooting depth. Lettuces normally have relatively shallow roots, reaching depths of 30cm or less. Cucumbers are sometimes described as shallow-rooting and sometimes as deep-rooting. However, studies show that when vegetable plants are grown together with a partner plant, they root differently – the roots spread out through the soil in a much more intensive way than when they are planted on their own. Furthermore, different types of vegetables have different soil nutrient requirements. The more varied the planting scheme, the easier it is to prevent nutrient deprivation in any one plant. Plants with high, moderate and low demands for nutrients can be grown together in companion planting. Heavy feeders usually absorb nutrients from the soil so effectively that plants with low nutrient requirements rarely suffer from overfeeding. Nevertheless, if you are using fertiliser, make sure that only the heavy feeders receive large amounts of fertiliser. Legumes such as peas and beans benefit from iron and zinc being released from the soil. In addition, legumes fix atmospheric nitrogen with the help of nitrogen-fixing bacteria in their root nodules, so the gardener does not have to apply as much nitrogen when fertilising. The legumes incorporate most of this nitrogen during growth, but after they have been harvested and the plants have died and started to decompose, valuable nitrogen is released back into the soil over a period of years. The vegetables that are grown after the legumes can then utilise this nitrogen.

3

4

Low demand for nutrients: provided that they are grown in soil rich in organic matter, these vegetables will not need fertiliser. Examples include dwarf French beans, dill, lamb's lettuce, carrot, parsley, radishes, rocket, winter purslane and sugarsnap peas.

Moderate demand for nutrients: these vegetables will need some fertiliser for growth. Examples include amaranth, Japanese greens (also called oriental greens), basil, endive, orache, Chinese mallow, butterhead lettuce, spring turnip, pak choi, loose-leaf lettuce, cos lettuce, beetroot, chives, summer purslane and spinach.

High demand for nutrients: these fast-growing, heavy feeders need regular applications of fertiliser. Examples include cape gooseberry, iceberg lettuce, cucumber, potato, kohl rabi, peppers, tomato and courgette.

NITROGEN

It is nitrogen that ensures green leaves. If the lower leaves of a plant turn yellow prematurely, this indicates a nitrogen deficiency. Anyone who has grown a tomato plant in a small pot without fertiliser knows what this looks like! If the plant cannot obtain enough nitrogen from the soil, it will draw nitrogen from the older leaves and into the youngest ones, and the plant will grow slowly.

Very green, fleshy leaves, such as those found on plants growing on manure heaps, indicate an excess of nitrogen. Although vegetables that contain too much nitrogen grow well, they are also very vulnerable to pests and fungal diseases because the plant tissue is so soft – a perfect snack for tiny vegetable lovers such as aphids. Tender, over-fertilised vegetables are delicious for us, too, but they can contain too much nitrate. Balanced fertilising is therefore important.

Nitrogen is one of around 20 essential elements that plants need to absorb in the right quantities if they are to develop properly and remain healthy. Most of these elements are available in the compost, as it consists of decomposed plant material.

OPTIMUM LIGHT CONDITIONS

The greater the area of leaf cover above the soil, the more sunlight is captured by the plants for photosynthesis, and the more produce we can harvest. In companion planting we strive to achieve complete coverage of the soil by plant foliage. Tall-growing plants stand among lower-growing ones, offering shade. In early summer, late-maturing plants are best planted in the gaps created after the early-ripening crops have been harvested. In August or September, winter vegetables can be sown below the late-maturing plants, thus ensuring a succession of harvests throughout the year. Intercropping, planting of green manure and greening the paths will leave very little open ground in which weeds can grow. The mulch should only be pulled back from the earth gradually in the spring to allow the ground to warm up in preparation for the first sowings.

RECIPROCAL ENCOURAGEMENT

Good neighbours planted together will yield more produce than they would if planted on their own. There are many reasons for this in addition to those mentioned earlier. Root exudates, such as saponins secreted by spinach roots, can help the neighbouring plants to take up nutrients. Strong smells confuse many pests, as when a mixture of odours lingers above a vegetable bed this makes it more difficult for them to find the right plant. If a pest wants to burrow its way from one cabbage root to the next in the soil, it will be deterred if there is a fat celeriac root presenting an obstacle to it. Herbs and other flowering plants attract beneficial insects with their fragrant blooms. Among these are hoverflies, lacewings and ladybirds. If they find enough pollen and nectar, they will lay their eggs among the aphids in the vegetables, and their larvae will then feed on the aphids.

GUARANTEED CROPS

With companion planting, there is always something to harvest. If one crop is eaten by slugs or snails, something else will continue to grow next to it. If there is a drought or a heat wave, cauliflower and scarlet runner beans will fail to

Yacons thrive in locations where the summers are long and hot. They are really tasty.

French marigolds are not only a good choice as companions for runner beans and tomatoes, but also look great in most planting schemes.

Spinach has shallow roots, so more nutrients are available for its deeper-rooted neighbours.

thrive, whereas yacons and tomatoes will positively flourish. Even when there are late frosts, gales or hailstorms, there are usually some vegetables that will make a good recovery and then continue to grow unaffected.

SUSTAINABILITY

Gardeners who use companion planting produce a large quantity of vegetables, fruit and herbs on a small area of land. In doing so, they maintain and improve soil fertility and provide habitats for many insects and other forms of wildlife. They are usually smallholders or hobby gardeners who engage in a lot of manual labour, as big machines and the large-scale use of pesticides and herbicides are not compatible with companion planting. As a result, a small-scale, species-rich landscape is created that often resembles a little paradise while at the same time producing a great variety of food.

FRENCH MARIGOLDS AND NEMATODES

Some nematodes are plant parasites, feeding on the roots of certain vegetables, whereas others are beneficial, breaking down organic matter and releasing nutrients. If only small numbers of parasitic nematodes are present they will cause little harm, but if they get the upper hand they will prevent healthy growth of vegetables. For example, nematodes of the genus *Pratylenchus* attack the roots of carrots and celeriac, stunting growth and causing forking of the root. They also attack the roots of beans, lettuces, onions, peas, black salsify, sweetcorn, potatoes, mustard, phacelia and strawberries, so crop rotation does not control these nematodes. The best way to combat them is to plant French marigolds (*Tagetes patula*), the roots of which produce a substance that inhibits the development and reproduction of parasitic nematodes. For this reason these flowers are frequently found in vegetable gardens with companion planting. However, other kinds of nematode, such as the sugarbeet nematode that affects beetroot, spinach and some brassicas, are not controlled by French marigolds, and are only eradicated by planting nematode-resistant types of white mustard as green manure.

In practice

Deciding what to grow in your mixed beds and staggered sowing is enjoyable and easy work. Digging over the ground and spreading compost is laborious at first, but less effort will be needed over time.

Surface composting is a significant contributor to the success of companion planting. The organic matter in the mulch is broken down by soil organisms and then serves either as fertiliser or as the basis for humus formation. Humus is our black gold – it makes the soil dark, loose and fertile.

FERTILISING

When a stinging nettle patch is converted into a vegetable plot there is no need to fertilise it, as the patch contains sufficient humus and nutrients. If the soil is light and hardly crumbles, add organic matter by applying compost or well-rotted manure. An initial application of 20 litres of compost per square metre is ideal in such locations. The quantities given in the box are recommended for 'normal' soils. I apply compost in the spring, rake it in lightly and then mulch immediately so that the soil organisms are protected. When sowing fine seeds, I do not remove any compost as there are many viable weed seeds in the compost just waiting for a glimpse of light to germinate. On my humus-rich vegetable plot, moderate and weak growers do not receive any compost – mulching is sufficient.

Few weeds germinate where the soil is mulched in summer. Pull single weeds out of the friable soil and leave them lying on top of the mulch as extra mulch. Reduce your workload by never allowing weeds to go to seed on the bed. When I hoe in dry weather in the spring the weeds wither, and they start to grow again when it rains.

WATER

Very little groundwater evaporates from the ground, as the mulch provides a protective layer that helps the soil to retain moisture. Moreover, as the mulch also excludes light, it provides optimum conditions for soil organisms. For this reason, except in prolonged hot dry weather you will normally only have to water what has been newly planted.

RECOMMENDED COMPOST QUANTITIES PER YEAR

HEAVY FEEDERS
9 litres/m²

MODERATE FEEDERS
5 litres/m²

LIGHT FEEDERS
0–3 litres/m²

A MINI MULCH ABC

MULCH: HOW THICK SHOULD IT BE?

Between the stages of sowing and seedling emergence, mulch is not needed – indeed, blackbirds are only too keen to push it aside in their hunt for earthworms, and in doing can sometimes uproot the young seedlings. If applying mulch, only a very small amount is necessary. Onions, lettuces and other tender plants prefer thin layers of mulch. On the paths, and between large plants, mulch should be at least 3–5cm thick. However, the mulch must remain as loose and air permeable as possible.

GRASS CUTTINGS: AN EXCELLENT NITROGEN SOURCE

Allow the clippings to dry out as much as possible before you use them as mulch, to avoid providing a haven for slugs. Grass clippings with seeds often lead to stubborn clumps of grass, so only use them in places where it's easy to pluck out germinating grasses.

WEEDS: A USEFUL MULCH

As the soil texture becomes looser through the addition of organic matter, the weeds become easier to pull up or hoe. In dry sunny weather you can leave them on the surface, where they will wither and form a highly effective mulch.

The softer and greener the mulch, the more nitrogen it has. In contrast, fresh wood chips or woody prunings draw nitrogen out as they rot down, which can make your plants nitrogen deficient. For this reason you should allow woody materials to rot down for several weeks before applying them.

HARVEST REMNANTS: SUPERFERTILISER

Crop residues that are not affected by pests or diseases can be left on the ground as mulch. Only coarse material that has not rotted down by the following spring, or that needs to be cleared to make space for new plants, should be placed on the compost heap.

LEAVES: THERMAL INSULATION

Be sure to collect leaves in the autumn. Slightly rotting leaves are ideal for covering the beds. To prevent the leaves from being blown away, weigh them down with some wet grass cuttings or friable soil. Leaves that do not rot down easily, such as sycamore, holly, walnut and eucalyptus, should not be put on the vegetable bed.

TYPICAL JOBS FOR SPRING

Wait for a dry spell to start on these tasks, as wet weather will quickly turn the soil into mud. The first thing to do is to rake the winter mulch to one side.

1. Once the ground has dried out, hoe the surface to a depth of 1cm. This causes the germination of weed seeds, which you can then remove with the hoe around 10 days later before you sow crops such as carrots.

2. In places where you plan to grow heavy feeders, increase nutrient levels by spreading a layer of compost 1–2cm thick over the bed after hoeing.

3. In other places, after hoeing, broadcast sow a green manure and hoe it in superficially. Many weed seedlings will also germinate here, but can be hoed out later together with the green manure.

4. For vegetable sowing, stretch out a string and make the furrow as deep as the recommended sowing depth so that the seeds lie on firm ground. Cover the seeds with fine crumbly soil.

5. When planting, make the planting hole deep enough for the roots to fit in comfortably. Water well afterwards. The plants may also require shading and mulch.

TYPICAL JOBS FOR AUTUMN

I like to mulch winter vegetables with leaves, which on frosty nights are a warm blanket for vegetables that are not completely frost-hardy.

1. Green manure that is susceptible to freezing does not need any attention.

2. Clean up other beds, weed and hoe them and place the coarse crop remnants on the compost. If the ground is very hard, loosen it with a garden fork by plunging the tines into the soil and moving them backwards and forwards, but not turning over the soil.

3. Where the soil is exposed, cover it with leaves, grass cuttings or similar mulching materials. Harvested remains that rot down well should be left on the row in which they have grown so that the crop rotation is adhered to. If only a light layer of mulch has been used, most of it should rot down over winter.

TEMPLATE BEDS FOR BEGINNERS

Ten tried and tested beginner beds throughout the year

On the following pages you will find 10 different planting schemes for companion planting. These beds look beautiful and will attract lots of pollinators to your garden while making your veg patch more productive.

All of the beds are 1.2m wide and are orientated in a north–south direction. Choose whatever length is most suitable for your site. The drawings show a potential 10-year plan if one takes crop rotation and the companion preferences of the plants into account. If you follow the plans in the order presented here the crop rotation will be correct. After year 10 the sequence starts again from the beginning.

CUSTOMISE AND ALLOW ROTATION

If you have 10 beds, or five half beds, you can simply let the plans rotate. Perhaps there are some types of vegetables that don't really appeal to you. You can simply replace these with other vegetables from the same plant family if they have the same space requirements and roughly the same growing period. For example, in a cool climate plants grow more slowly and March sowing is not possible. With the assistance of the tables on pages 43, 63 and 88–91, and some experience of growing vegetables, you can tailor the plans to meet your requirements. As soon as your plan is providing the optimum solution for your requirements you can simply rotate the beds.

LABOUR-SAVING TIPS

— Mark the corners of your beds with solid wooden pegs so that you do not have to measure them out again every year. In addition, keep 10cm of ground free at the lawn edge so that one wheel of the lawn mower can roll over the ground. I cut the edges of the lawn with the strimmer line set perpendicularly, and afterwards I go over them once with the hoe.
— The paths between the beds are always covered with grass cuttings or

A snail fence provides very good protection against snails so long as you first remove all of the slimy creatures from the enclosed area inside.

leaves, as is the uncultivated soil, so hardly any weed seeds are able to germinate.

— Once you have sown or planted up rows of vegetables, mark the front and back with thin sticks. For sowing it is helpful to stretch out a string (see also page 18), because completely straight rows are easier to hoe and also you will be able to identify the weeds more quickly as they will be very obvious. In addition, keep a written record of all the crops that you have sown – including the date for each type – in your bed plan so that in the weeks and years to come you will be able to check what you sowed where.

— To combat snails, I have laid a snailproof fence round one-third of my vegetable beds, which rotates in line with my cultivation plan. In the remaining two-thirds of the beds the snails struggle to find anything that they like to eat.

— Be hypervigilant about weeds – always hoe or hand weed them before they run to seed, and when the weather is dry you can leave them lying between the rows of vegetables, to be devoured by your friends the earthworms. If you allow certain weeds to run to seed you will then have a great deal of weeding to do in the years that follow; a similar situation occurs if you allow many types of vegetable to run to seed. Only apply compost where germinating seedlings are going to be given free rein afterwards. This is not a problem between cabbages, celeriac, leeks or courgettes, as you can just hoe out the many seedlings. However, if you apply compost before sowing carrots, you will be constantly searching for carrot seedlings in the small green jungle that develops.

NETTLE SLURRY

Fill up to two-thirds of a large plastic bucket with stinging nettle tops, water and some compost, and put it in a warm place. Stir it daily for two to three weeks and then use the clear liquid diluted 1:10 for vegetables that are heavy feeders.

CELERIAC-LEEK-BROCCOLI BED

PLANTS IN THE BED

Broccoli
Celeriac
Leeks

This bed remains under its mulch blanket until mid-May. This means that, from March onwards, you can toss on mulch from neighbouring beds that is no longer needed.

WHAT TO DO WHEN

March/April When it is dry enough, briefly pull the mulch to one side, add a 2cm layer of compost and then pull the mulch back over the bed so that the soil organisms in the compost are protected.

Mid-May Mark up the celeriac row 20cm in from the top edge, the broccoli row 25cm in from the bottom edge and the leek row 35cm away from the celeriac row. Plant the celeriac spaced 40cm apart within the row, the leeks spaced 20cm apart and the broccoli spaced 50cm apart. When planting, open up the mulch blanket only at the location where you intend to plant, and then pull the mulch back thickly around the plant, but leaving a space around the stem to prevent rotting and ensure that all the leaves receive light. Then water carefully.

July to mid-August Since all the plants in this bed are heavy feeders, over the summer they should be fertilised once or twice with nettle slurry (see page 23). These plants also appreciate fast-rotting mulch made

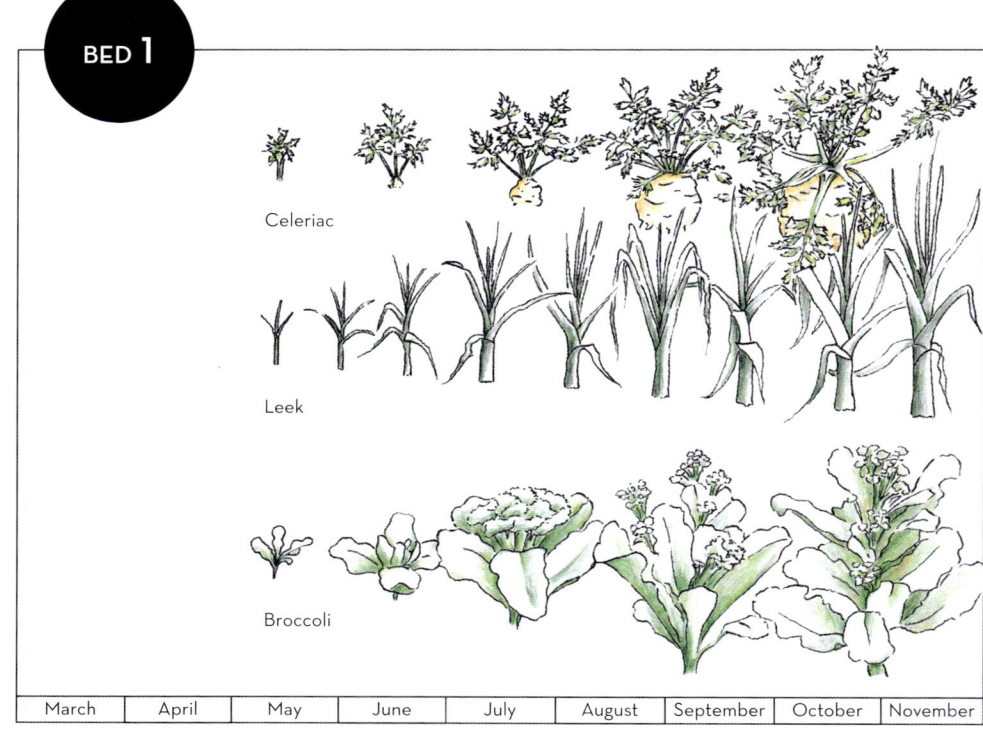

BED 1

1. If you harvest the florets carefully with a sharp knife, the heritage broccoli variety 'Calabrese' will continue to produce new side florets until the first hard frost.

2. Celeriac, leeks and broccoli grow well together.

from comfrey or nettle leaves. I harvest the broccoli florets throughout the summer before the buds separate (once they turn yellow they lose their flavour).

October Celeriac survives the first light night-time frosts under a covering of leaves. For leeks, the timing of harvesting will depend on the frost hardiness of the individual variety. Winter leeks can be harvested throughout the winter. The cut and come again broccoli varieties can be harvested right up until they are destroyed by frost, and some varieties can tolerate several degrees below freezing. In late October or early November, mulch the bed thickly with leaves.

GOOD PARTNERS

In scientific trials in Switzerland, higher yields were obtained by growing leeks and celeriac together. In my garden, too, the pair simply seem to belong together. Celeriac also deters cabbage white butterflies, the broccoli keeps celeriac rust and leek pests at bay, and the leeks repel clouded drab moth caterpillars from the broccoli.

Celeriac This is planted with the crown exposed above the surface of the soil, to avoid the development of side roots. Celeriac requires plenty of water. Once the bulbs have been harvested, the leaves can be dried, pulverised and mixed with salt to form a herby seasoning.

Leeks When planting, cut the roots back as little as possible – they should fit into the planting hole with the roots extended outward. Plant leeks deep so that they form long white shafts; I create a channel and then plant them using a weeding trowel. However, all of the leaves must stand proud of the soil. I pour soil in to close up the channel later when I am weeding, and then heap up the soil a little.

Cut and come again broccoli After the first floret has developed, heritage broccoli varieties form small florets over and over again in the leaf axils, so amazing yields can be had from these varieties, particularly in the autumn. In contrast, many of the modern, commercially grown varieties form an enormous giant floret initially, but so few florets thereafter that it is not worth continuing to harvest the plants.

LETTUCE-BEANS-BRASSICA BED

PLANTS IN THE BED

Dwarf beans
Japanese greens
Kale
Kohl rabi
Lamb's lettuce
Leaf lettuce
Leeks
Loose-leaf lettuce
Radishes
Savory
Spinach
Winter purslane

Three harvests from one bed? Go for it! At the end of March, harvest the last leek and pull the mulch blanket off the bed to allow the ground to dry out and warm up.

WHAT TO DO WHEN

April At the beginning of April, sow Japanese greens and spinach. For both of these, sow them 10cm from the edge, and 25cm further in sow the lettuce rows. In the loose-leaf lettuce row, leave gaps so that you can sow radishes in the row as well. You can do the same with leaf lettuces. Plant early kohl rabi varieties in mid-April in the middle of the bed, spacing plants 50cm apart within the row, with 50cm between rows.

May By the end of May in milder locations you can be regularly harvesting tender leaves for colourful salads – spinach, leaf lettuce, loose-leaf lettuces and Japanese greens can all be used as cut and come again crops if you cut them above the heart of the plant. From mid-May, sow the bean row between the lettuces and 20cm from the edge. Leave some room in the bean row and sow savory in between. As soon as the beans germinate, the spinach, lettuces and Japanese greens will have to make room for the beans, which will eventually take up all the space. Mulch lightly with grass clippings.

June In early June, plant kale and Brussel sprouts spaced 50cm apart in the gaps between the kohl rabi plants, and add about 1 litre of compost per plant. You can start to harvest the kohl rabi this month. The middle row can now tolerate being mulched. Chard could be used as an alternative to kale between the kohl rabi plants, but in this case fertiliser should not be added. Mulch the beans carefully.

September After the beans have been harvested, sow winter purslane and lamb's lettuce for winter harvesting. Keep the middle kale row well mulched.

Winter On frost-free days you can harvest kale, Brussel sprouts, lamb's lettuce and winter purslane.

GOOD PARTNERS

Lettuce keeps striped flea beetles away from brassicas such as radishes, Japanese greens and kohl rabi. The rows of lettuces will protect the bean seedlings from cold winds. The savory not only repels the black bean aphid but will also give the beans a wonderful aroma if you add a few sprigs of it during cooking.

Japanese greens are colourful and delicious almost all year round.

TEMPLATE BEDS FOR BEGINNERS

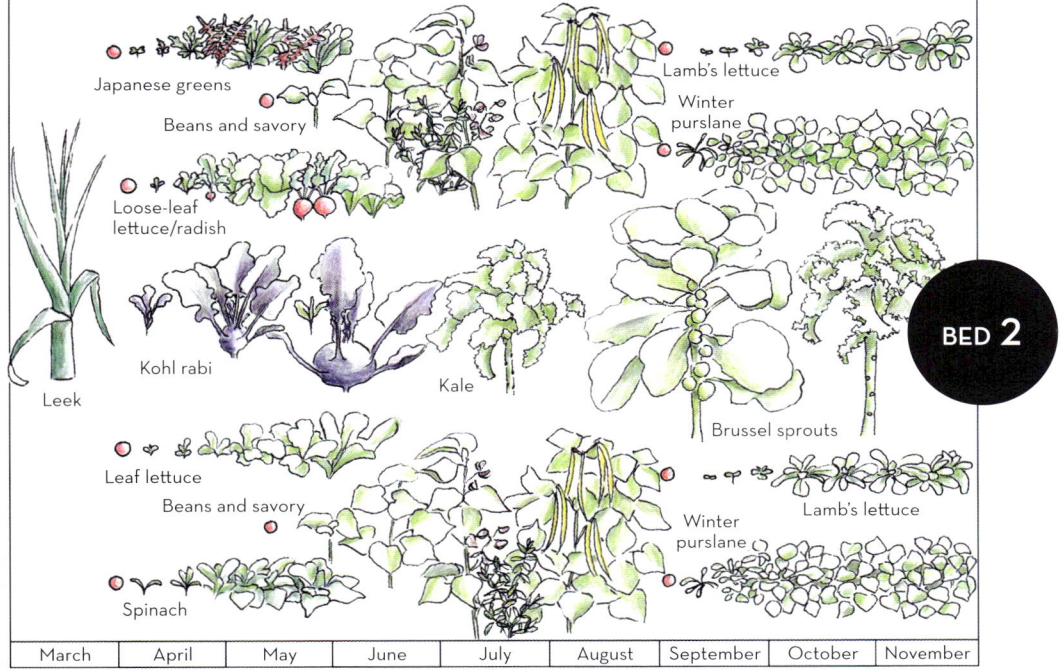

The tender-leaved savory keeps aphids away from the dwarf beans.

Japanese greens These are available in colourful mixes. Tastewise, the spectrum ranges from ultra hot to very mild. These greens are harvested and used like leaf lettuce. I prefer to cultivate the fast-growing and mild-flavoured mizuna form. The spring and autumn sowings taste fantastic. Autumn sowings can be harvested over a long period in mild winters.

Dwarf beans If you like beans but are not fond of brassicas, you can put runner beans in this bed and omit the Brussel sprouts and kale, as runner beans take up more space. I have found the robust dwarf bean variety 'Maxi' to be very high yielding. When I sow a bunch of savory next to roughly every fifth bush, there are hardly any aphids. This does not work for runner beans, however, as they grow too tall.

Savory Put in a stick to mark the spot where you sow this, so that you do not accidentally hoe up the tiny seedlings.

Kale and Brussels sprouts When buying young plants choose frost-hardy, late varieties if you would like to harvest throughout the winter. For kale, I love the tall 'East Friesian Palm' variety, which I grow from seed myself. You might also like to include a red kale. In late Brussels sprouts varieties, you can start harvesting from the bottom and work your way up the stem over the course of the winter.

Radishes There are three important things to remember: select the right variety for the time of year, always water evenly, and plant with leaf lettuces which will protect the radishes from the striped flea beetle.

TOMATO-CABBAGE BED

PLANTS IN THE BED

Basil
Brussels sprouts
Butterhead lettuce
Cabbage varieties
(white cabbage,
pointed cabbage,
red cabbage, savoy
cabbage)
French marigolds
Garlic
Lamb's lettuce
Parsley
Pot marigolds
Tomatoes
Winter purslane

'Pinching out' (i.e. removing by hand) the small side shoots in the leaf axils of staked tomatoes. Do this in dry weather.

This can be harvested up to the end of April. In early May, hoe up all of the winter crops when the ground is dry. Apart from the cabbage stalks, most of the plant material can remain on the bed as mulch.

WHAT TO DO WHEN

Mid-May Mark out the tomato row 35cm from the edge, the brassica row 30cm from the edge and the lettuce row in the middle of the first two rows. Plant the various late cabbage varieties at spacings of 40–50cm, according to the variety, applying 1 litre of compost per plant. When planting the heads of lettuce, space them 30cm apart. Plant the tomatoes beside their stakes, spacing the plants 60cm apart and using 2 litres of compost per plant. In front of the tomatoes, at the edge of the bed, you can put in single plants of basil (use 30cm spacing), garlic (10cm spacing), parsley (20cm spacing), pot marigold (20cm spacing) and low-growing French marigold (25cm spacing). Now water and mulch.

July The first tomatoes are ripening – a happy sight! Regularly tie the tomato plants in to the stakes and pinch out the side shoots. As soon as the lettuce has been harvested, the cabbage and tomatoes will spread out. Apply nettle slurry and nutritious mulch.

October As soon as the cabbages start to split, they are ripe and must be harvested quickly. Most cabbage varieties tolerate light frosts, and can be covered with leaves on the occasional frosty night. Savoy cabbage is particularly hardy. Gather all of the tomatoes in before the first frost – the green ones will ripen really well at 20°C indoors, and usually only very small tomatoes will not ripen.

Winter Add the cabbage stalks and tomato stems to the compost. Cover the bed with a protective layer of leaves. Weigh down the leaves with grass cuttings or crumbly soil.

GOOD PARTNERS

Tomatoes deter cabbage pests, and if you plant some mugwort in with the cabbage it will repel cabbage white butterflies. Pot marigolds reduce early blight in tomatoes. In scientific trials, tomatoes grew well when planted with basil, garlic, cabbages, heads of lettuce and pot marigolds. Together, these vegetables produced higher yields than when they were grown as single crops.

Cabbage varieties Plant late varieties of white cabbage, pointed cabbage, red cabbage or savoy cabbage. When planting, take account of the varying space requirements of these varieties. This is where some experience helps. For example, the pointed cabbage, which according to seed packets needs less space, is the one that requires most room in my garden. In contrast, I can plant red cabbage and savoy cabbage a little closer together.

Tomatoes Out in the open, use varieties that are suitable for outdoor cultivation, and which are resistant to tomato blight, such as the cooking tomato 'De Barao', the cherry tomato 'Primabella' or the wild tomato 'Red Marble'. Any potatoes should be planted as far away as possible, to reduce the risk of tomatoes becoming infected by leaf blight spores. In rainy weather the spores would then germinate and attack the tomato leaves. Due to our warmer summers and more robust varieties, growing tomatoes outdoors is a viable option.

Basil Plant a basil variety suitable for outdoor cultivation – basil plants from the supermarket are unsuitable for this. Wild basil grows best in my garden.

Pot marigolds These are resilient and easy to grow, and you can also harvest them as cut flowers and for their seeds. I use the petals to make teas and salves.

Heads of lettuce You don't need to buy limp leaves from the supermarket – it is easy to grow your own young plants yourself, and only takes four weeks (see pages 60 and 68).

The roots of French marigolds produce a substance that inhibits the development and reproduction of nematodes (see page 15), which damage tomato plants by boring into their roots.

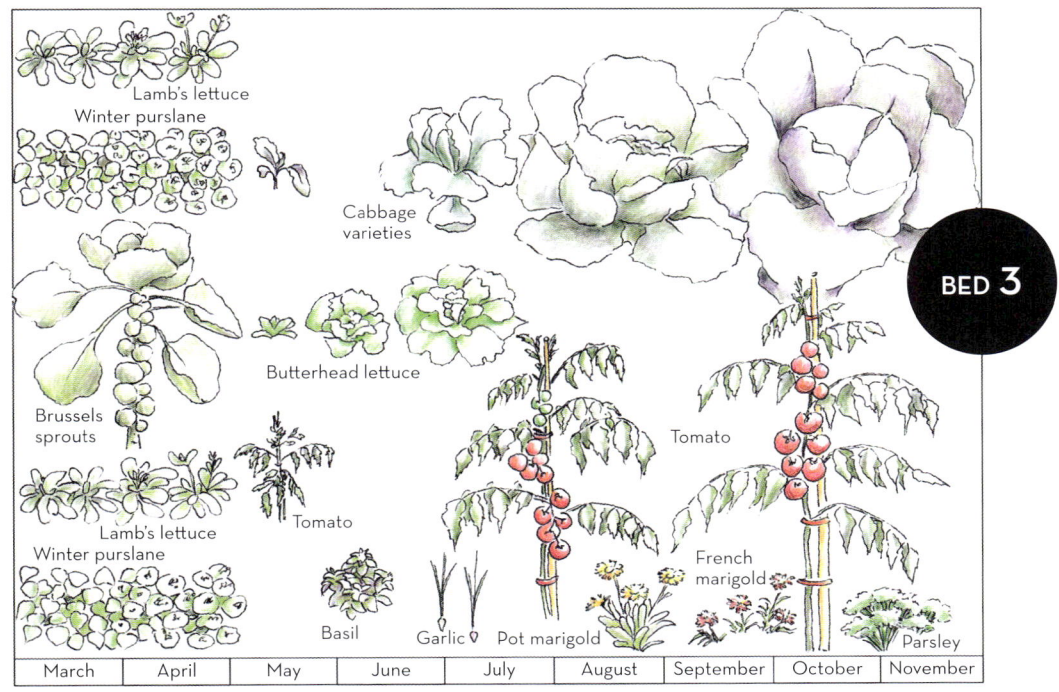

CUCUMBER-BEETROOT-ONION BED

PLANTS IN THE BED

Abyssinian cabbage
Basil
Beetroot
Cucumbers
Endive
Loose-leaf lettuce
Onions
Rocket
Spinach

If the cucumbers grow well, this bed will quickly turn into a dense jungle. If they fail to thrive, you can either do another sowing or replace the cucumbers with Florence fennel in July.

WHAT TO DO WHEN

April In early April, pull the leaves off the bed and mark up the onion row and the beetroot row, each of these two rows being 15cm from the edge, with the cucumber row in the centre and the loose-leaf lettuce rows in between. You can plant various kinds of loose-leaf lettuce at 30cm intervals. In mid-April, plant the onion sets at 4cm intervals. The top third of the onions should stand proud of the soil. At the end of April, hoe the bed flat and sow the beetroot.

Mid-May For the cucumbers, sow three seeds at a time at 30cm intervals and mark each planting spot with a small stick. Place a basil plant instead of a cucumber in every fifth planting spot. Spread about 1.5 litres of compost around each of the cucumber planting sites. The cucumbers sprawl enthusiastically across the ground in my garden. If you want to have a support, you can also build a frame for them. With the exception of the onions, the bed can now be mulched.

August From July to mid-August the cucumbers also appreciate the application of nettle slurry. After the onion harvest, in what was the onion row you can plant winter endive up to mid-August at 40cm intervals, if the cucumbers allow space for this.

September By now the cucumbers will be succumbing to mildew. Clear them away and sow spinach, Abyssinian cabbage and rocket in several rows (depending on your personal requirements), and also possibly lamb's lettuce.

October Harvest the beetroot before the first hard frost. Carry on harvesting the lettuces until they are destroyed by hard frosts. The winter spinach will last through to spring.

GOOD PARTNERS

Cucumbers and lettuces get on well together, as the lettuces protect the sensitive cucumber seeds from the wind and can be harvested when the cucumber vines take over the bed. Basil prevents both cucumber mildew and whitefly, and it also attracts beneficial insects, so the

Beetroot, cucumber with basil, and lettuce with crow garlic.

TEMPLATE BEDS FOR BEGINNERS

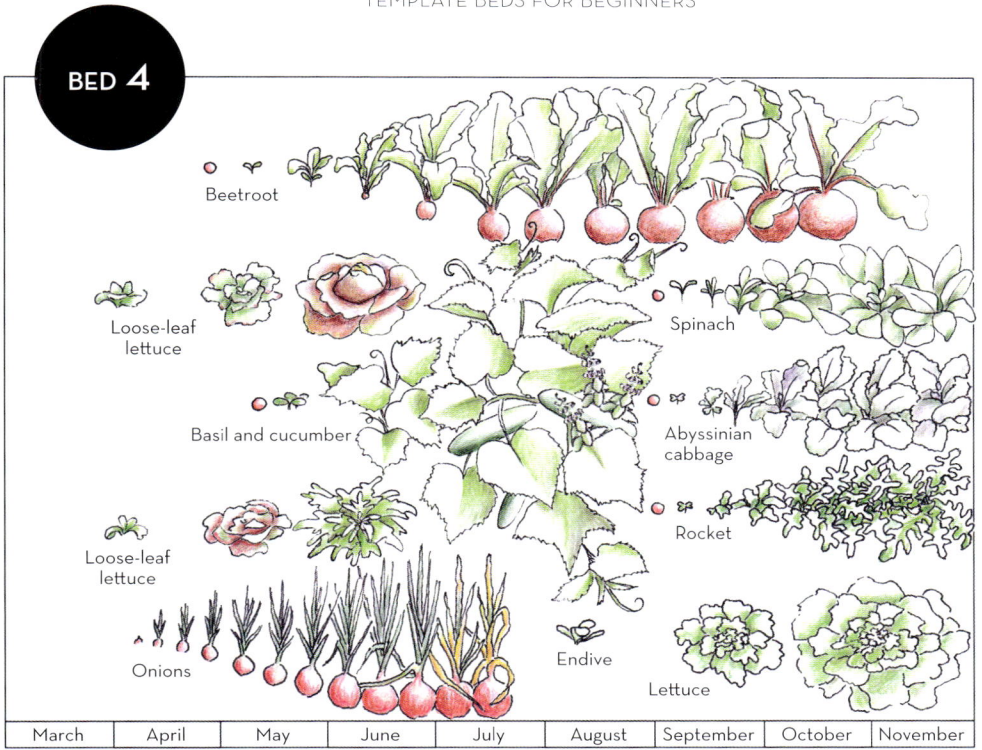

cucumbers give better yields. In scientific trials, onions and cucumbers grown together produced higher yields than either crop grown separately, and the same was true for rocket grown with endive.

Beetroot In my garden, beetroot grows throughout the summer. If you have planted beetroot seedballs – each of which contains several seeds – you will need to thin out the plants throughout the summer. When thinning out, you should harvest baby beetroot the size of golf balls, as these 'baby beets' are particularly tender and delicious.

Cucumber If you struggle with cucumbers, try growing the 'Tanja' variety. Cucumbers grow best if you sow them *in situ* rather than starting them off on a window sill. They like warm sheltered conditions but hate cold winds and being watered with cold water. The soil should be loose, rich in humus and evenly damp – a case for a beautiful layer of mulch.

Onion When buying onion sets, make sure that they are no more than 1.5cm in diameter, as larger sets bolt easily in the summer. Even though they are native to the steppes, onions do need to be watered regularly when growing. Only when they are ripening do they need to be dry.

Abyssinian cabbage If you sow this fast-growing cabbage species only in the autumn, instead of flowering it will provide large numbers of tender leaves for salads. Harvest the leaves when they are 6–8cm long. They have a tender, nutty but cabbage-like taste.

Once planted, the pointed end of each onion should still be clearly visible.

CARROT-SUGARSNAP PEA BED

PLANTS IN THE BED

Carrots
Chinese mallow
Cress
Dill
Radishes
Sugarsnap peas
Winter purslane

Carrots take several weeks to germinate, during which time they can get lost among faster-germinating weeds. For this reason it is best to prepare for sowing carrots, where possible, by hoeing twice.

WHAT TO DO WHEN

March As soon as the ground has dried out, pull the mulch and the remnants of harvested plants on to the paths and hoe over the ground to a depth of 1cm. The hoeing will stimulate weed seeds to germinate. If you are early enough, you can broadcast sow mustard alongside the carrot rows.

April At the beginning of April, sow the sugarsnap peas in the middle of the bed and push twigs vertically into the ground at 15cm intervals, to act as supports. In the second week of April, hoe the carrot rows and the ground around them to a depth of 1cm when it is dry and sunny, so that the weeds and mustard seedlings dry out afterwards. In mid-April, sow the carrot rows at a distance of 20cm from the edge, and also sow radish marker seeds at approximately 20cm intervals, so that you can hoe safely before the carrot seeds germinate. Sow dill seed between the carrots at intervals of about 12cm, and finally

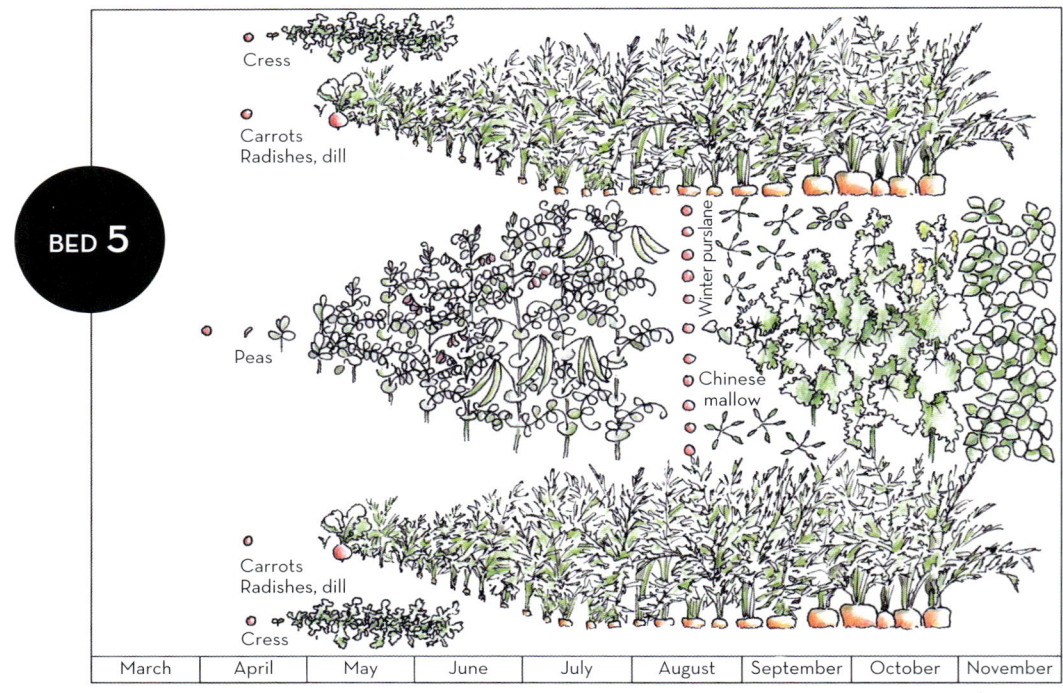

BED 5

scatter some tansy powder (see page 73) or shield fern powder over the carrot seeds. On the outside of the bed, 5cm from the edge, sow a row of garden cress.

May Some peas need to be encouraged to climb initially, but they will soon romp away. Harvest the radish and dill leaves for salad as soon as the carrots need the space. The cress should also never be allowed to overcrowd the carrots, but you can allow it to flower here and there so that you can harvest the seeds.

August As soon as the peas have been harvested, plant a row of Chinese mallow in the middle of the bed, and sow winter purslane widely around this. It is also possible to sow overwintering spinach in this location, but wait until September to do this.

GOOD PARTNERS

Dill promotes the germination of carrots and provides shade for the tender seedlings. Peas fix atmospheric nitrogen from the soil and loosen up the soil texture, which later benefits the carrots and follow-on crops. Peas grow better next to the carrots. Tansy and shield fern keep insects away but must only go on to the bed in powder form. The smell of the cress repels carrot fly.

Carrot I grow late variety 'Rothild', which is ideal for storage. I harvest it at the beginning of November when the cellar is cold enough for storing it. The early varieties of carrots are smaller, but make delicious snacks when eaten raw in high summer.

Dill This is very popular in companion planting, but in many old vegetable gardens it will not grow because fungi in the soil cause the seedlings to perish. Crop rotation is extremely important for dill, as it is for all umbellifers.

Sugarsnap peas A 60–80cm tall variety can be grown here, the pods of which ripen within two to three weeks. Shorter varieties ripen faster. Taller varieties take longer to mature and require better support. The pods are normally harvested when the seeds become prominent. I like to leave them on the plant a little longer and then shell the sweet seeds.

Winter purslane This small companion plant requires temperatures below 12°C for germination, so you need to be patient while waiting for the first seedlings to appear at the end of summer. However, once germinated it grows rapidly and will keep your salad bowls full throughout the winter. It is a great self-seeder, but can easily be hoed out when it is in the wrong place.

Cress For use in sandwiches this should be harvested before the flower stems start to develop. Let some plants go to seed so that you can grow fresh cress over the winter.

1. Sugarsnap peas need climbing supports and some initial encouragement to climb.

2. Radishes sown as markers make it very easy to identify the carrot rows before the carrots finally germinate three weeks or more after sowing, and you can hoe earlier.

COURGETTE-SWEETCORN BED

PLANTS IN THE BED

Basil
Courgette
Runner beans
Spinach
Summer purslane
Sweetcorn
White mustard
Winter purslane

In the middle of the bed the winter purslane from last year will still be growing. You can harvest the leaves on a cut and come again basis until the end of April to pep up your winter salads.

WHAT TO DO WHEN

March On the first enticing spring days, sow the spinach rows at a distance of 15cm from the edge.

April From mid-April, start three courgette plants on a sunny window sill. Use two to three seeds per 12cm pot, and allow all the seedlings to grow. If the winter purslane is still dense, make sure that you hoe it out by the end of April so that it can rot down – the root fibres that it leaves behind are very persistent. I do allow the odd plant to grow and even run to seed, taking the risk that I will later have to pluck out many small seedlings from among the strawberries. As our family only needs three courgette plants, I cultivate runner beans in the north part of the bed (not shown), erecting the framework for these in April. I plant kohl rabi, and sow spinach and lettuce between the poles.

May At the start of the second week of May, plant the sweetcorn in the middle of the bed in clumps (three seeds spaced 20cm apart in a triangle). The clumps should be spaced 90cm apart. Now and then leave one sowing area free, which you can then plant up with basil in mid-May. Also in mid-May plant the courgettes in the middle of the bed, spaced 90cm apart, between the sweetcorn seedlings. For the sweetcorn and courgettes apply 2 litres of compost and extensive mulch around every planting site. At the edge of the bed, at the level of the sweetcorn, sow some summer purslane.

September When you clear the bed at the end of September, there will still be time to sow mustard, so long as the runner bean plants are not too dense.

GOOD PARTNERS

The sweetcorn provides the courgettes with some protection from the wind and sun, and the courgettes shade the soil and keep it cool for the sweetcorn. In trials, sweetcorn and courgettes produced higher yields when grown together than separately. Basil reduces the impact of powdery mildew on the courgettes and ensures good fertilisation. Sweetcorn and runner

Sweetcorn and courgettes complement each other beautifully.

TEMPLATE BEDS FOR BEGINNERS

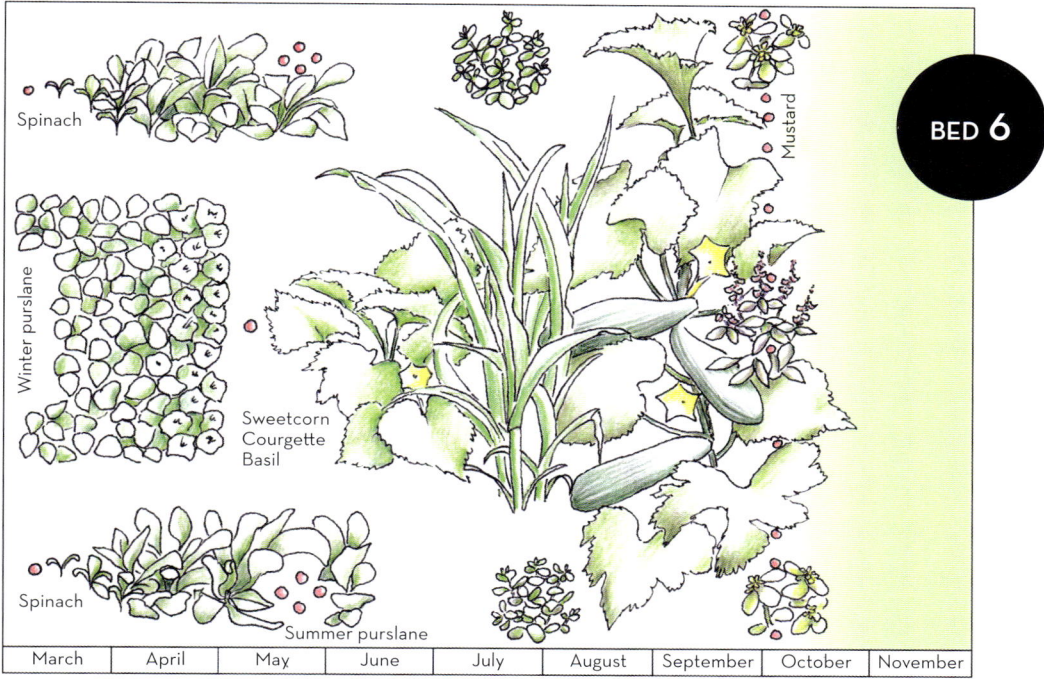

beans are a dream pairing (shown growing together in Bed 1 on page 66, and they can also be tried out in the north end of this bed).

Spinach In very warm regions it is best not to grow any spinach over the summer, as it bolts too quickly. For the spring and autumn sowings plus overwintering I recommend the 'Matador' variety, but do try other varieties, too, as their suitability is very dependent on location and climate.

Courgettes I always select the early, green-fruiting varieties as they produce the fastest harvest. The variety 'Zuboda' is really mildew resistant in the autumn where I live. Cultivating young plants is very easy – all you need is a sunny south-facing window sill. Once the courgettes have been hardened off and planted, shade them with leafy twigs, as young courgette leaves are very delicate. Frequent spraying with water often speeds up root establishment.

Sweetcorn The sweetcorn kernels contain more sugar than fodder corn cobs, so it is well worth growing your own. However, if fodder corn pollen from surrounding fields gets into the mix during wind pollination, the kernels will be less sweet than they would otherwise be. During storage the sugar is quickly converted to starch, so it is best to consume the cobs immediately after harvesting.

Summer purslane This small drought-resistant salad herb grows like a weed and self-seeds. The really young leaves have the best flavour, and green varieties thrive best.

POTATO-BROAD BEAN-STRAWBERRY BED

PLANTS IN THE BED

Basil
Broad beans
Coriander
Dill
Endive
Lamb's lettuce
Mustard
Phacelia
Potatoes
Strawberries

Phacelia provides broad beans with very effective protection against bean aphids.

If you do not want strawberries you can shorten the crop rotation here – sow green manure and then get going with the first bed.

WHAT TO DO WHEN

March As soon as the sunny spring weather arrives and the ground feels drier, pull apart the mulch for the bean row and push the broad bean seeds into the soil 25cm from the edge of the bed. In the potato row add a 2cm thick layer of compost under the mulch. Towards the end of March, place medium-sized potatoes in a flat crate and chit them at 12–15°C on a well-lit but not sunny window sill.

April Sow some phacelia and dill with the broad beans. They should be sown loosely around the beans so as not to overcrowd them. In late April, place the chitted potatoes in the soil 35cm from the edge, spaced at 30cm intervals and about 5cm deep, but do not earth them up immediately.

May If frost is forecast, hoe some soil over the potato leaves. Once the potato plants are 15cm high, earth them up by pulling the soil up from both sides onto the plants. Repeat this process once again later. Then scatter coriander seeds. From mid-May you can plant some basil with the broad beans.

Mid-August The broad beans and potatoes will now have been harvested. Plant the strawberry plants at intervals of 30cm in a row 25cm from the edge. Between each pair of strawberry plants sow a patch the size of a soup bowl with mustard seed, which can be hoed out when the plants are 10cm high. Sow two rows of lamb's lettuce at 10cm and 40cm from the edge, respectively. In the middle of the bed, plant the winter endive at intervals of 40cm.

GOOD PARTNERS

Broad beans fix their own nitrogen in their root nodules, so there will be plenty of nitrogen available for the potatoes. In scientific trials, phacelia, dill and basil were found to keep aphids away from broad beans fairly successfully. Coriander is said to improve the aroma of potatoes. This is well worth trying as it looks pretty anyway. Mustard, lamb's lettuce and endive protect the soil and they buffer the young strawberry plants against cold winds, creating a sheltered microclimate in which they can thrive.

Potatoes Varieties vary in their resistance to pests and diseases. This is very apparent when several different varieties are grown next to each other. It is a good idea to research the optimum variety for your conditions and preferences. As potatoes are susceptible to viruses, you cannot carry on replanting them year after year. Every few years you will need to eat them all up and purchase new, healthy seed potatoes.

Lamb's lettuce As lamb's lettuce is not related to any other vegetable group, it is ideal for fitting into the crop rotation in autumn as green

manure. I often broadcast sow it as early as mid-August under large plants such as tomatoes and runner beans, before they are cleared away. If you sow frost-hardy varieties of lamb's lettuce from mid-August to September, you can harvest them all winter long, right up until April. In spring you can leave some plants in the bed so that they run to seed.

Broad beans These are related to the field bean, have plump seeds and thrive in a damp, cool climate. Warm dry conditions cause problems with aphids. I squash squadrons of the sometimes gigantic infestations of aphids with my fingers, but an even better solution would be to attract ladybirds – a natural predator of aphids. Harvest the beans while they are still unripe, shell them and cook them. You can also harvest them when ripe, but you then have to render them edible again by soaking and cooking them for a long time.

When potatoes are being earthed up on sunny days, the weeds growing alongside them get their comeuppance.

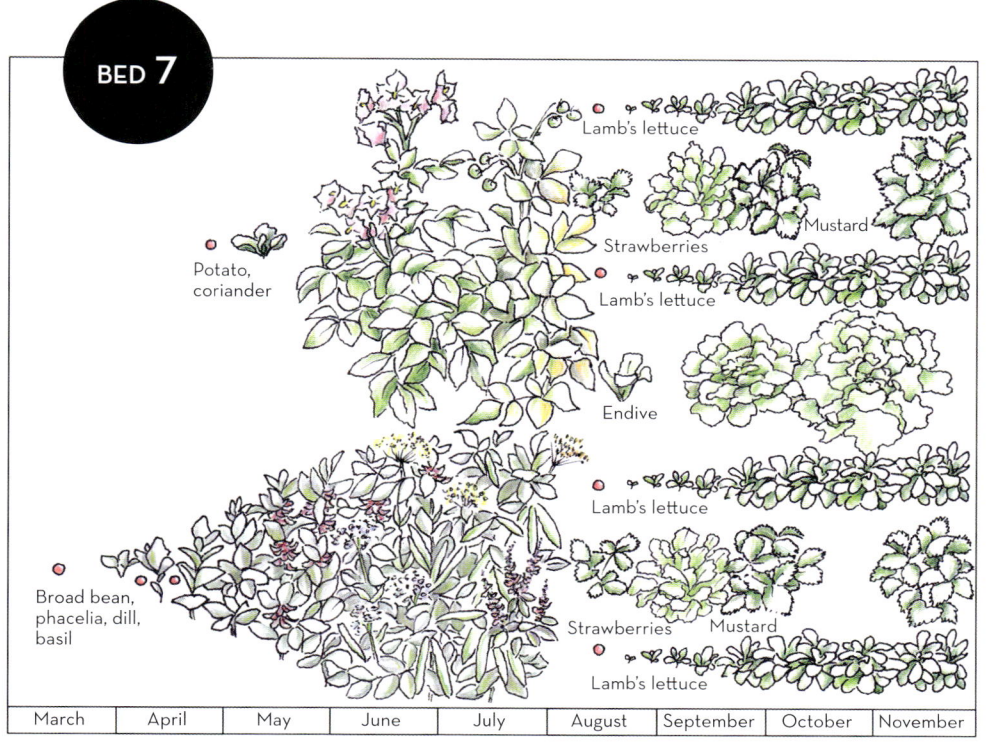

STRAWBERRY-GARLIC-FRENCH MARIGOLD BED

PLANTS IN THE BED

French marigolds
Garlic
Onions
Strawberries
Snail-scarer mix: pot marigolds, chervil, coriander, chamomile

You can very successfully keep snails at bay by sowing a mixture of French marigold, pot marigold, chervil, coriander and chamomile in the middle row of the bed.

WHAT TO DO WHEN

March Harvest the outer rows of lamb's lettuce (from Bed 7) so that you can plant a row of rocambole cloves (also called hardneck garlic or serpent garlic) 8cm from the edge, 4cm deep and spaced 20cm apart.

April Between each pair of strawberry plants put in one onion set so that two-thirds of it protrudes above the soil surface. If snails are a problem, sow the middle row of the bed with my tried and tested snail-scarer mix – pot marigolds, chervil, coriander and chamomile.

May If snails are out at night, in mid-May you can plant French marigolds in the central row. I use a small variety, 20cm tall, with single flowers so that they will attract bees and butterflies, and I keep the marigolds in check so that they never impede the growth of the strawberries. Also mulch with dry chopped straw, which has the added benefit of preventing rain and mud from splashing the strawberry fruits,

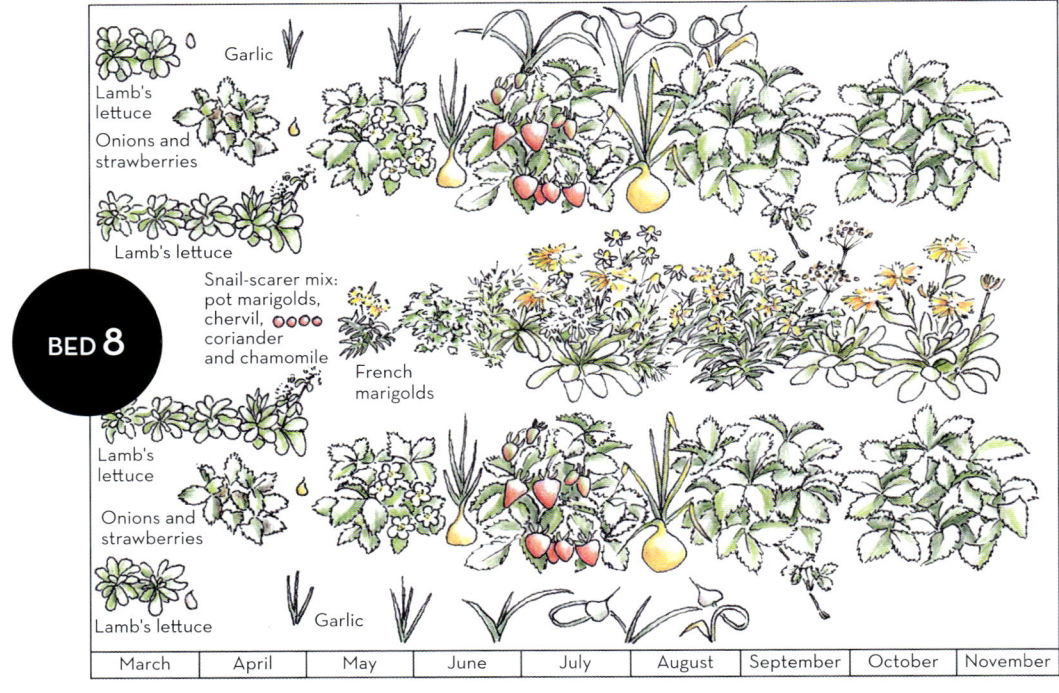

thereby reducing the risk of grey mould. Fine hedge trimmings are a suitable alternative, with the exception of yew and thuja, which are toxic. Garlic and onions are not particularly fond of mulch, so only mulch the garlic row thinly.

August Remove superfluous runners from the strawberries, and position the rest so that they close up the gaps between the strawberry plants in the row. In addition, harvest the garlic and onions, add compost to enrich the soil, and apply mulch.

GOOD PARTNERS

Members of the onion family, such as garlic, onions, leeks, chives and garlic chives, reduce the likelihood that the strawberries will become affected by grey mould. When grown together in trials, strawberries and plants belonging to the onion family produced higher yields than when they were grown separately. Garlic can protect strawberries from the strawberry mite, and French marigolds suppress harmful parasitic nematodes in the soil.

Strawberries I choose varieties grown organically by professional growers. My favourites are the early variety 'Elvira' and the mid- to late-season variety 'Polka', both of which are robust and high-yielding. If you have several different varieties, pollination is greatly improved. Good ventilation is important for reducing the risk of fungal diseases. After harvesting, cut off any diseased leaves and dispose of them – do not compost, as they may affect your other plants.

Garlic Rocambole grows better in our climate than true garlic. It forms looping flower stems on which small cormels form. You can buy the cloves for planting from a seed merchant, or a gardener in your neighbourhood may have some.

French marigolds The roots of French marigolds produce a substance that inhibits the development and reproduction of parasitic nematodes. If parasitic pratylenchus nematodes pierce the roots of strawberry plants, they will inhibit the growth of the strawberries and multiply. These nematodes also affect many other edible crops (see page 15), roses and even weeds, such as dandelions, among many other plants. If French marigolds alone are grown in a bed, the number of nematodes can drop by up to 95 per cent in one year. However, these marigolds are also veritable slug magnets!

1. The rocambole helps to keep the development of grey mould on the strawberries in check. If you plant the small cormels it will be two years before you can harvest proper garlic cloves again.

2. In damp weather, grey mould causes juicy strawberry fruits to rot.

STRAWBERRY-GARLIC BED

PLANTS IN THE BED

Chives
Garlic
Garlic chives
Strawberries
White mustard

The strawberries will now require almost the whole bed, so only minor modification is possible in the middle row with plants from the onion family.

WHAT TO DO WHEN

March Weed thoroughly around the strawberry plants. Fill about two-thirds of the middle row with garlic cloves spaced 10cm apart. Plant up the remaining third of the middle row with chives and garlic chives spaced 20cm apart. If there is no mulch left, add more around the strawberry plants, though try to avoid mulching the middle row.

May Mulch the strawberries well, but if possible do not use too much fresh, fast-rotting material, as an excess of nutrients makes them prone to white spot and leaf spot disease.

June Before harvesting, mulch with straw. During this year's harvest, mark the plants with the highest yields and the healthiest ones with the best fruit. Over the course of the next few weeks, take runners from these plants. To do this, after harvesting sink a 10cm pot beneath each of the selected plants and fill it with humus-rich soil. Then wait for the strongest runners from the best plants to take root.

August In mid-August, pinch off the new small strawberry plants from the mother plants and move them to their

BED 9

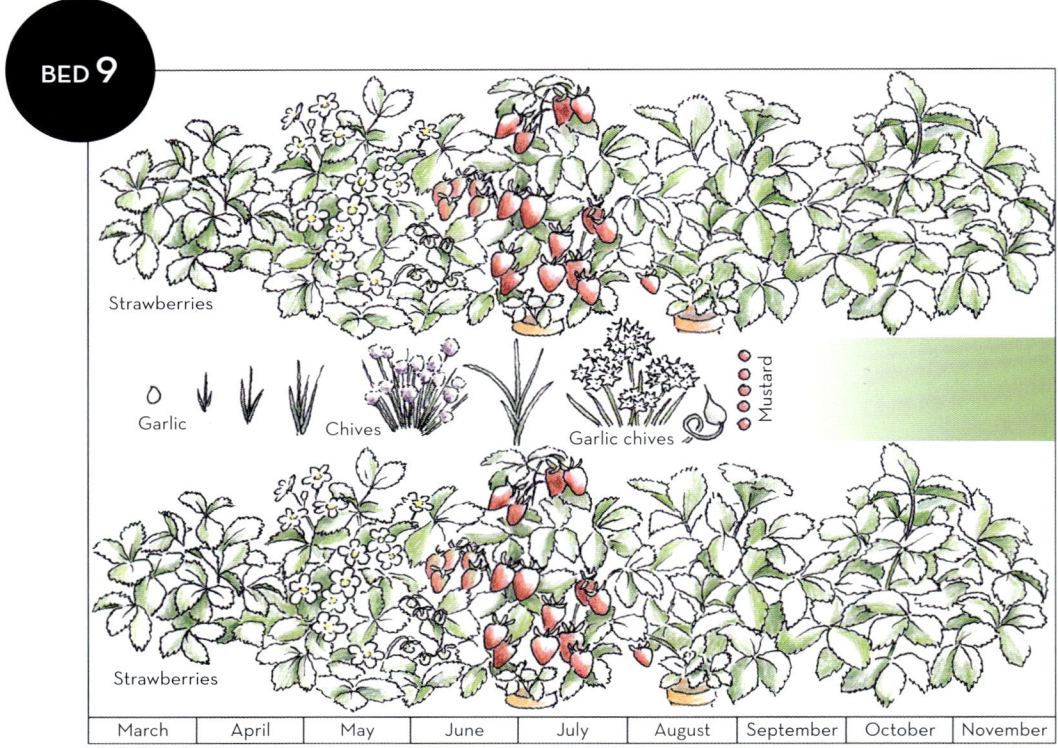

1. A layer of straw under the fruit provides more effective protection against grey mould than rocambole. The netting keeps the birds out.

2. After harvesting, the plants form strong runners which quickly take root.

3. Allow the runners from the plants with the best fruit to take root in sunken pots. After developing root balls while in the pots, they grow on much better when re-planted into the new bed.

---

new homes. Again, remove all superfluous runners, as the quality of the fruit will be impaired if it is covered by dense foliage. If you end up with too many strawberry plants for your bed then they can make a fantastic gift for family and friends. Where I cut off old and diseased leaves, I sow some mustard around the strawberries. I then pluck this out when it is about 10cm tall and leave it lying as mulch. This adds life and variety to the soil. You can also harvest the garlic – it tastes best when freshly harvested.

GOOD PARTNERS

Chives Every few years these need to be re-located. When re-planting, always divide them.

Garlic chives These plants are extremely robust, have wonderful flowers and readily run to seed. The leaves have a mild garlic flavour.

STRAWBERRY-GREEN MANURE BED

PLANTS IN THE BED

Strawberries
Green manure (e.g. phacelia or lyme grass)

If the strawberries are still producing good yields, you can leave them in place for another year. However, strawberry plants do show a marked decline in yield in their fourth year.

WHAT TO DO WHEN

Weeding and mulching are always necessary. Dig up the chives and garlic chives, and plant them somewhere else because of the crop rotation (see Bed 9, page 40). They work well as companion plants in a flower bed.

July After the strawberry harvest, clear the strawberry plants, hoe thoroughly and sow a green manure. Phacelia and buckwheat are particularly suitable with regard to crop rotations, as they are not related to the vegetables. Moreover, it is very easy to harvest seeds from the buckwheat if you sow it in early May and allow the seeds to mature. From a few square metres you can quickly harvest up to 1 kg of seeds, which can be used to sow green manure for several years to come. Flax, borage, lyme grass, Chinese mallow and sorghum, or a mixture of any of these, will also work well here as green manure. All of these plants perish in the frosts over winter and leave behind a wonderfully crumbly soil for starting afresh with the first bed.

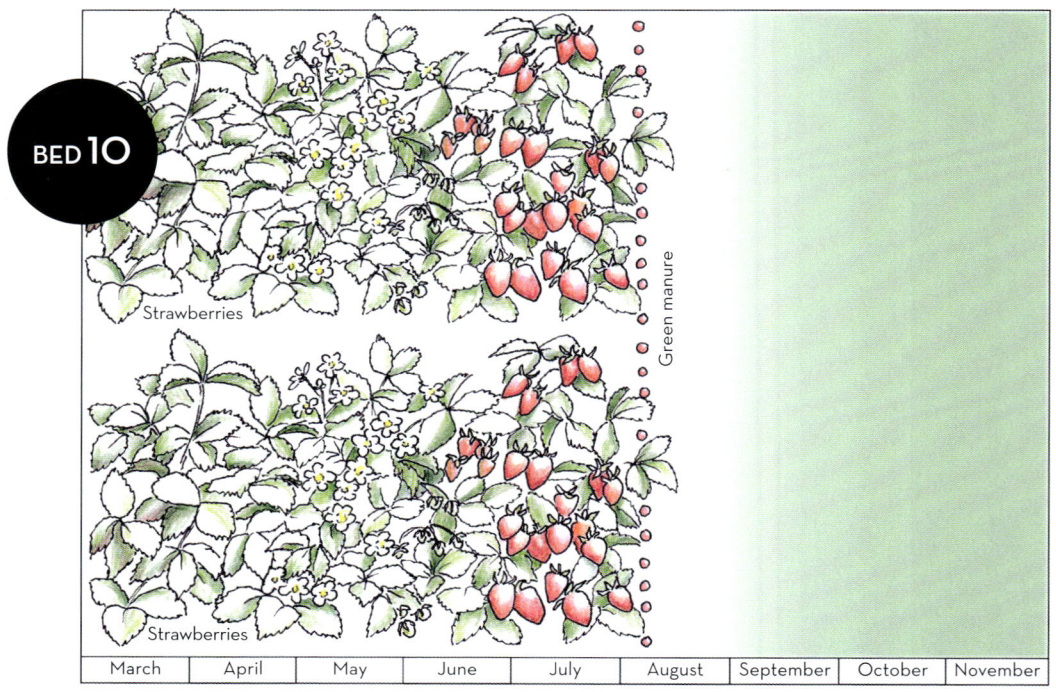

PLANT FAMILIES

Vegetables from the same family often grow poorly together and infect each other with diseases. The families listed in the table below are seriously affected.

PLANT FAMILY	CHARACTERISTICS AND FAMILY MEMBERS
Umbellifers	A typical umbellifer has a dense umbrella-shaped flower head. Carrot fly is a pest of all umbellifers. Members of this plant family include dill, fennel, chervil, coriander, caraway, carrot, parsnip, parsley and celeriac.
Amaranth family	The flowers are generally small, and are normally pollinated by the wind. Beet leaf miner and viruses are problematic. Members of this family include amaranth, orache, Swiss chard, giant goosefoot, beetroot and spinach.
Brassica family (also called crucifers)	The flowers are characteristically in the form of a cross with four petals, and the plants often have a distinct cabbage-like, hot flavour. The main pests are slugs and snails, cabbage whitefly, cabbage root fly, cabbage stem flea beetle, and the caterpillars of diamond-back moth, cabbage moth and cabbage white butterfly. Clubroot severely affects brassicas. Members of this family include cabbage, Chinese cabbage, cress, pak choi, turnips, radish, horseradish, rocket and mustard.
Legume family	The typical butterfly-like flower of legumes has a large upper standard petal with a boat-shaped keel below and wings at the sides. Legumes have root nodules that can fix atmospheric nitrogen from the soil. Viral and fungal diseases are common. Members of this family include beans, peas, clover, lentils and vetch.
Nightshade family	The flowers have five petals, often fused to form a funnel-shaped tube. Pests include slugs, snails and potato cyst nematodes. The main disease is blight, which affects both potatoes and tomatoes, and potato blackleg and viruses can also be problematic. Members of this family include sweet and cayenne peppers, chillies, aubergine, potatoes and tomatoes.
Onion family	Most of these plants have an onion-like smell, long smooth leaves, and fat flower buds encased in two parchment-like leaves. The main pests are onion fly, leek miner and leek moth. Onion white rot and neck rot and leek rust can be a problem. Members of this family include onions, spring onions, garlic, leeks, shallots, chives and garlic chives.

MIXED-ROW CULTIVATION WITH CLOVER PATHS

In mixed-row cultivation there are many vegetable rows in a large bed. The row plan you will find on the following three double-page spreads remains the same, but moves 30cm further on each year so that the crop rotation is followed correctly. You can walk barefoot on the soft white clover paths, as the clover does not produce flowers in the first year. Here are some basic tips in advance.

Bed preparation In March, when the soil has dried out, rake over the entire bed and deposit the mulch and harvested plant remains next to the vegetable area. Often the soil under the mulch is so loose that it will not be necessary to hoe. Otherwise, hoe it over to a depth of 1cm. With a furrow opener, mark a flat furrow every 20cm. Sow clover in the space between the rows, followed by a 120cm area of bed, and then another 20cm-wide clover path and so on.

Fixed markings Mark the start of the bed area with two sturdy sticks so that every year you have the same fixed measuring points. At the front and back of the bed area there should be a little leeway so that you can slide the clover paths along if it makes sense to do so.

Clover paths In March, stretch a string along the clover path, broadcast sow the clover seeds (at a rate of $2g/m^2$) on to the path and carefully rake them in. If it is a cold spring, it will be a while before you can walk on the clover paths, but the seedlings are tough and can tolerate light loads. If necessary, I lay boards down, but mostly I balance carefully between the crops sown. Over the summer, white clover can fix atmospheric nitrogen at a rate of $20g$ nitrogen/m^2, which means that you save on fertiliser (20g nitrogen is equivalent to approximately 4kg of well-rotted manure). The clover also mitigates the footfall damage. In late autumn or, at the very latest, in March, hoe the clover away, as in the following year the clover path is to grow 30cm further on.

Spinach rows In March I sow a neat, straight row of spinach 40cm from the clover paths. In cooler northern regions or at higher altitudes, sowing at the beginning of March might be too early, as it can still be cold for several weeks. In April and May the spinach protects the small vegetable seedlings from cold winds and provides a source of fresh greens. As soon as it gets in the way or starts to flower, I hoe it out and leave it to lie on the ground, spreading old mulch from the winter over it. The soft spinach leaves and roots provide a real feast for soil organisms. The high saponin content of spinach is said to help other plants to take up nutrients. After it has been hoed out, the spinach rows in summer can be used for surface composting as well as for walking on and watering.

Autumn jobs When the mixed cultivation rows have been harvested, up until mid-September it is worth adding another green manure in the form of white mustard. Later in the year, loosen up the soil only where necessary with a garden fork, and mulch the rows that are now becoming free. From October everything should be covered with a colourful blanket of leaves.

1. In spring the clover on the path is still rather limited in its growth.

2. In summer, after trimming with the strimmer, the clover is growing rampantly. Plucking means more work, but produces more mulch.

ROW PLAN WITH SIX CLOVER PATHS

The work guidelines for the clover paths and for the two spinach rows situated between them can be found on page 44. The tasks you need to do in the 17 vegetable rows are described in the following text. In addition, all vegetable rows that include heavy feeders should be given a little compost or well-rotted manure in March or at the time of planting, and a large amount of nutritious mulch over the summer.

Clover Path 1 see page 44

Row 1: Lettuce-kohl rabi In mid-April, plant early kohl rabi and early heads of lettuce alternately every 20cm. A few dill seeds should be sown with these. When gaps are caused by harvesting, once again plant or sow kohl rabi, radish, horseradish, dill or lettuce; in summer, plant varieties that do not bolt (e.g. cos lettuces), from July sugarloaf chicory and winter endive. Around mid-August is the last opportunity for kohl rabi. Rocket, white turnips, autumn turnips and Japanese greens fit between the lettuces from August onwards. The lettuces protect the brassicas from cabbage stem flea beetle.

Spinach see page 44

Row 2: Phacelia-dwarf beans From April, broadcast sow phacelia. From mid-May, hoe areas to sow within the phacelia and then sow the dwarf French beans. When doing so, leave about 15cm of extra space after every fourth to fifth cluster and sow a cluster of savory. Mark it with a stick so that you do not take it out when hoeing. Weed the phacelia so that the beans do not get cramped. Many dwarf French bean varieties, such as 'Maxi', produce flowers again after the first harvest and go on to produce a second crop of beans. The dwarf beans benefit from having the lettuces as neighbours. In September, broadcast sow phacelia.

Spinach see page 44

Row 3: Beetroot-Swiss chard-coriander From March, broadcast sow white mustard. From mid-April, hoe the row for sowing and then sow Swiss chard in one part of the row and beetroot in the other. Both of these crops produce higher yields when grown together with dwarf French beans. If you sow the beetroot widely, there will be room between them for a few coriander seeds. The coriander flowers well in the summer – I harvest the seeds when they turn brown and then cut the plants down so that the beetroot can develop fully.

Clover Path 2 see page 44

Row 4: Dill-lettuce Here lettuces and dill can grow until courgettes or cucumbers from row 5 start to predominate. In March, sow some leaf lettuce, and then sow dill at the end of March. From mid-April, plant heads of lettuce and loose-leaf lettuce at intervals of 25–30cm. If gaps open up in the cucumber or courgette jungle at the beginning of August, plant sugarloaf chicory and radicchio. Cucumbers, courgettes and lettuces grow happily together and produce higher yields than when they are grown separately.

Spinach see page 44

Row 5: Crimson clover-cucumber-courgette-lamb's lettuce In late March or early April, broadcast sow crimson clover, and from mid-May sow cucumbers in one part of the row. For this, hoe the crimson clover to one side at the site for sowing and mark this with sticks after sowing. Here and there plant up a sowing site with basil, and do not plant cucumber seeds there. Plant up the other part of the row with courgettes spaced 80cm apart (two plants are sufficient for a family). The crimson clover can be left to grow so long as it does not take over the ground around the cucumbers and courgettes. From mid-August to mid-September, broadcast sow lamb's lettuce between the cucumbers and courgettes.

TEMPLATE BEDS FOR BEGINNERS

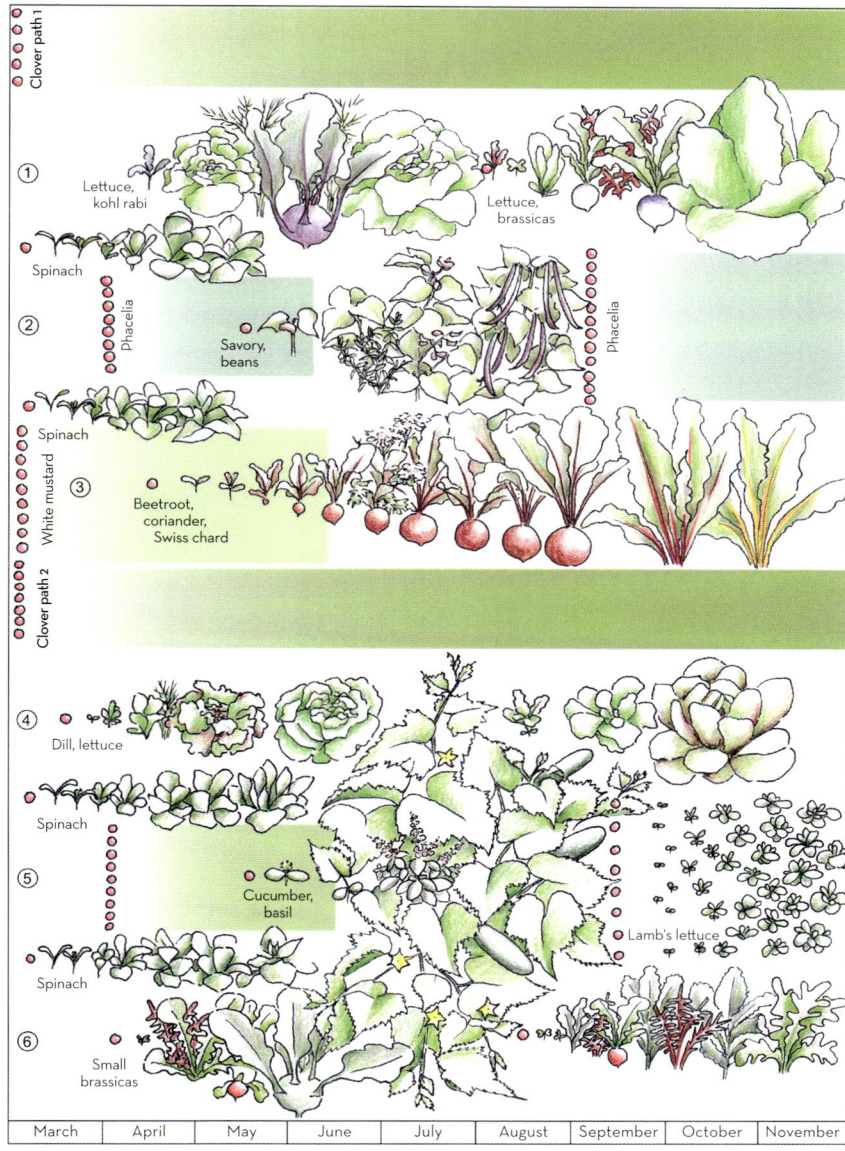

Spinach see page 44

Row 6: Brassicas such as Japanese greens, rocket, kohl rabi, horseradish and radishes In late March or early April, divide up the row and sow something different in every section. Japanese greens, rocket, kohl rabi or other small brassicas are suitable. These are still initially protected from cabbage stem flea beetle by the spinach. In summer, the cucumbers and courgettes grow rampantly over the row. From mid-August there may be space again for autumn turnips, Japanese greens, spinach and radishes. However, if cucumbers and courgettes only make room for other crops later, you can still sow rocket, radishes and Abyssinian cabbage up until early September.

Clover Path 3 see page 44

Row 7: Carrots for storing In April, sow late carrots for storing, which you can harvest in October and November before the first hard frost, as under a layer of leaves they should survive light frosts. Planted near the leeks, they are fairly well protected from carrot fly, and in turn they protect the leeks from onion fly and leek moth. In trials, carrots and leeks grown together produced higher yields than when they were grown separately.

Spinach see page 44

Row 8: White mustard–winter leek In March, broadcast sow white mustard, which you can then hoe out around mid-May. As soon as you can buy young plants, plant winter leeks with a spacing of 20cm. You can harvest these from October to March if they do not freeze completely and then thaw too many times. A thin layer of leaves will protect them from hard frosts and winter sun. They do even better under the snow. In this row, autumn or summer leeks would also do well. Summer leeks can be planted as early as the beginning of April and harvested from mid-July. Onions or shallots would also be feasible here, with a follow-on sowing of autumn spinach or lamb's lettuce.

Spinach see page 44

Row 9: Crimson clover–early cabbage–late cabbage In late March or early April, broadcast sow crimson clover between the spinach row and the clover path. From mid-April, plant an early cabbage variety at 60cm intervals in gaps freed up by hoeing between the clover. From the end of May, plant a late cabbage variety (e.g. 'Marner Lagerweiss') between the early cabbage plants, and weed out the crimson clover if it is getting in the way. Alternatively, plant only spring cabbage at 40cm intervals. If, from June, you leave the bottom leaf rosettes in place, shoots will sprout from the stalk, and you can allow three or four strong shoots to remain. From these, small heads of cabbage will form once again, which for the most part survive mild winters undamaged, allowing fresh cabbage to be harvested throughout the winter.

Clover Path 4 see page 44

Row 10: Early carrots–dill–radishes–early beans At the beginning of April, sow an early variety of carrot (e.g. 'Nantes 2') with a little dill and radish as a marker sowing. To deter carrot fly, sprinkle tansy powder over the seeds. When the carrot seedlings are about 5cm tall, sprinkle them with tansy powder again. Once the carrots have been harvested you can in mid-July sow an early variety of dwarf French bean (e.g. 'Speedy', 'Saxa' or 'Maxi').

Spinach see page 44

Row 11: Onion sets–small brassicas such as horseradish, radishes, rocket and Japanese greens In April, plant a double row of onion sets. The two rows should be 20cm apart, and within each row the onions should be spaced 5–6cm apart. Once they have been placed in the ground the upper third of each onion should protrude above the soil surface. After the onions have been harvested, sow small brassicas such as horseradish, radishes, Abyssinian cabbage, Japanese greens, autumn turnips and rocket, as well as lamb's lettuce and spinach planted in between. Narrow crops such as lamb's lettuce can be planted in a double row.

Spinach see page 44

Row 12: Lettuces such as leaf, loose-leaf, iceberg, cos and lamb's lettuce Here there is room for an endless supply of lettuce. In spring, sow leaf and loose-leaf lettuces, in summer sow iceberg, cos, Batavia or frisée lettuces, and from August plant endive and sugarloaf chicory or sow lamb's lettuce. Mix and match what you grow according to your requirements. Between adjacent heads of lettuce that are almost ready for harvesting sow new lettuces, so that at the time of harvesting there are already young plants growing between the ripe heads of lettuce. If your sowings are denser than what you actually need, you can also remove young plants from here at any time and transfer them into other rows.

TEMPLATE BEDS FOR BEGINNERS

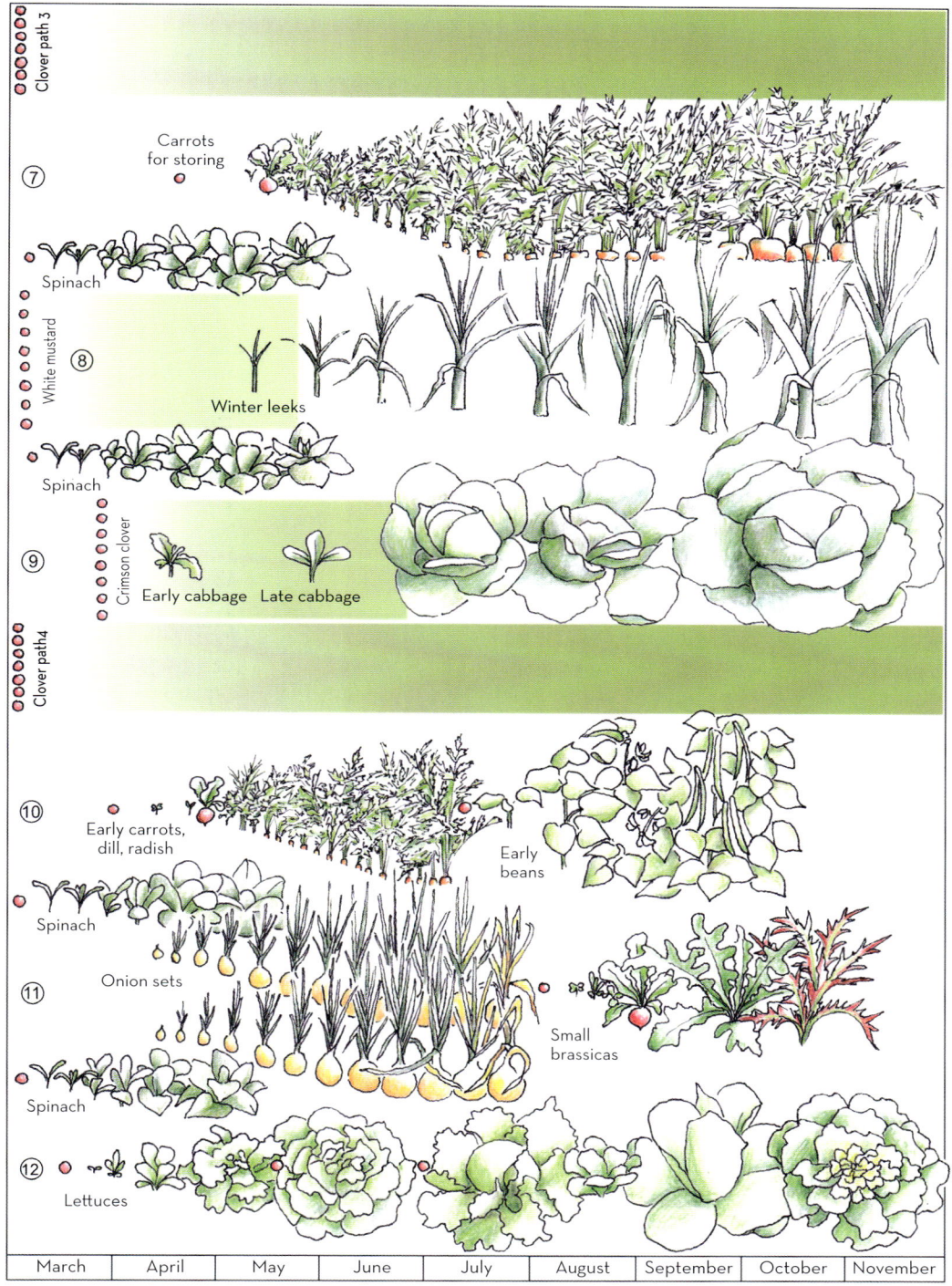

Clover Path 5 see page 44

Row 13: Sugarsnap peas–Chinese mallow In early April, sow sugarsnap peas. After they have germinated, hoe them in dry weather and place branches along the row for them to climb up. When the peas have been harvested, sow Chinese mallow. This grows rapidly, which means that you can harvest tender leaves right through to the first hard frost. They are delicious in a salad. Taller pea varieties, which will need a sturdier frame, would give you a longer pea harvest. After this there would still be time to grow lamb's lettuce. Alternatively, you could sow Chinese mallow directly next to the peas even during the pea harvest, and then clear away the peas carefully.

Spinach see page 44

Row 14: Broccoli–celeriac In mid-May, plant celeriac and broccoli alternately at 40cm intervals. Celery and cauliflower would also fit into the row. Once it has been harvested, you can replace the cauliflower with rocket or a small brassica, or sow phacelia. The brassica and celeriac benefit each other as the celeriac drives away the cabbage white butterfly while the brassica suppresses fungal diseases, especially rust, on the celeriac. Once the peas have been harvested, the heavy feeders on this row benefit from the nitrogen that the peas have accumulated.

Spinach see page 44

Row 15: Garlic–lamb's lettuce From mid-March, plant a row of garlic cloves (rocambole) 4cm deep at intervals of 10cm. In one part of the row put in the small bulbils that grow on the top of the rocambole plant, placed somewhat closer together. By summer they will have grown into cherry-sized, tender bulblets which you can then dig out and put back next spring. They develop into healthy garlic bulbs with many thick cloves. In scientific trials, garlic produced higher yields when grown together with broccoli and cauliflower. After you have harvested the garlic, broadcast sow lamb's lettuce.

Clover Path 6 see page 44

Row 16: Pot marigold–sweetcorn–broad bean Pollination in sweetcorn is most successful when the plants are growing close together, so at each site sow four seeds spaced 20cm apart from each other in a square. The squares are located in the middle of a row, which here is 25cm from the clover path. Aim to have one sweetcorn clump per metre, and mark it up in March. Between the clumps there is room for a 40cm-long row of broad beans or pot marigolds, both of which can be sown in March. Sow the pot marigolds over the locations for the sweetcorn clumps and then weed them out in May wherever they are in the way. From the end of the first week of May you can sow the sweetcorn, which from the outset should never be crowded by the marigolds. In trials, when sweetcorn was grown together with broad beans or potatoes it produced higher yields.

Field beans Instead of spinach, sow field beans here at a distance of 60cm from the clover path. Hoe them out once they have started to flower.

Row 17: Potatoes–winter purslane or green manure such as phacelia or lyme grass At the end of March, chit medium-sized potatoes at 12–15°C in flat crates on a well-lit windowsill out of direct sunlight. At the beginning of May, place the potatoes between the two rows of field beans. Put them in the ground at a depth of about 4cm and spaced 30cm apart. When the plants are about 15cm tall, earth them up and at the same time hoe out the weeds that are growing alongside. When weeds start to germinate alongside once more, earth up the potato plants again. Then mulch them thickly. Only harvest the potatoes after the foliage has died back completely. You can then broadcast sow a green manure or winter purslane, such as phacelia with lyme grass.

Field beans Sow field beans 10cm from the clover path. Hoe them out once they have started to flower.

TEMPLATE BEDS FOR BEGINNERS

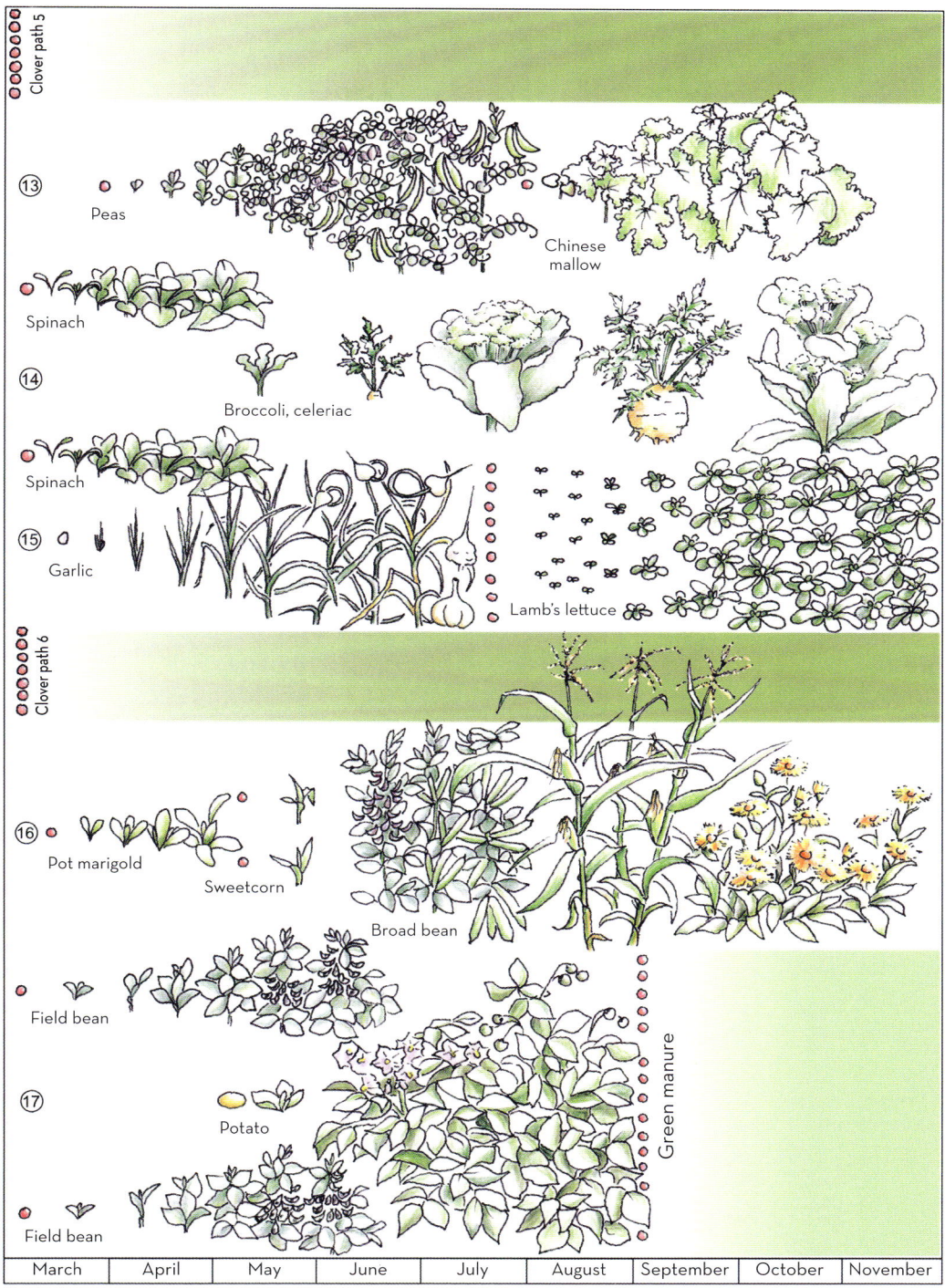

Companion plants in containers

Companion planting is especially important in containers because space is limited both above and below the soil surface, and they are often planted more densely than beds.

All containers require good drainage so that there is never any standing water in the compost. Containers with a water reservoir are ideal, especially in the hottest weeks of summer. The best type of compost for plants with low nutrient requirements is herb compost. Plants with a moderate or high demand for nutrients grow well in multipurpose compost enriched with fertiliser. Heavy feeders need liquid fertiliser every two weeks in the main growing season. If large containers are used the soil can be enriched with well-rotted compost, from which nutrients are released by the activity of soil organisms. However, in smaller containers there are insufficient organisms in the soil for this. Warm, sheltered locations are ideal for most vegetable species and varieties that can tolerate the strong midday sun. However, dark-coloured containers can become too hot for some of them.

SUMMER HARVEST TUBS
Tub dimensions: 25 x 30 x 70cm

Scarlet tub In March, sow baby leaf lettuce. In mid-May, sow scarlet runner beans (no. 1) next to the plant support, and at the front in the centre put a one-year-old savory plant (no. 3). In the front corners plant one creeping rosemary (no. 2) and one nasturtium plant (no. 4).

Cucumber tub In March, sow spinach at the back. In April, place three kohl rabi at the front and sow leaf chicory (no. 3) in between. In mid-May, place two cucumber plants at the back next to the trellis (no. 1), with one wild basil plant in between (no. 4). After the kohl rabi has been harvested, sow dill (no. 2) in the gaps, and from September sow winter purslane under the cucumbers.

TEMPLATE BEDS FOR BEGINNERS

SUMMER HARVEST TUB
Tub dimensions: 25 x 30 x 70cm

Paradise tub In March, sow two rows of leaf lettuce together with radish. In mid-May, plant one tomato plant (no. 1), one wild basil (no. 2), two nasturtium plants (no. 3) and one pot marigold (no. 4). From September, undersow lamb's lettuce.

BALCONY BOX FOR NIBBLING
Tub dimensions: 25 x 30 x 70cm

Vitamin box In March, sow leaf lettuce together with radish. In June, plant two butterhead lettuces (no. 2) and sow baby beets (no. 3) and dill (no. 1) in between. At the end of August, sow rocket, Chinese cabbage, winter purslane and lamb's lettuce.

BALCONY BOX FOR NIBBLING
Box length: 60cm

Gourmet box Plant two wild strawberry plants (no. 1), one garlic-chives plant (no. 2) and one lemon balm plant (no. 3).

Herb box Plant one basil plant (no. 1), one parsley plant (no. 2), one chives plant (no. 3) and one great burnet plant (no. 4).

RAISED BEDS FOR PLENTIFUL FRESH VEGETABLES

A four-year crop rotation is created in these two beds if you divide the raised-bed plans down the middle. In the first two years, the second side should mirror the first, then you can use the other raised bed in the following two years. In the plans the spring vegetables are shown in green type, the summer vegetables in black and the autumn vegetables in blue. If you use the plans in raised beds measuring 120 × 200cm, the plants will be tightly packed so there will be a lot of overhang and you will have to harvest vigilantly. In beds measuring 140 × 220cm you can fit in an extra plant here and there.

1. Tomato half: In March, broadcast sow white mustard (not shown), but keep the loose-leaf lettuce rows empty. From the beginning of April, plant eight loose-leaf lettuces and sow dill in between. Around the second week of May, hoe out the mustard and leave it lying to act as mulch. By mid-May the bed will have become very full. Plant two bush tomatoes and sow pot marigolds in between, which can then be allowed to grow on until they start to get in the way. Do not let them run to seed. Then plant the parsley, removing any loose-leaf lettuce that is in the way (the lettuce and parsley are incompatible). Now sow the beans with some savory, and plant one broccoli, one early cauliflower, two celery and one nasturtium plant. From August/September broadcast sow winter purslane and lamb's lettuce among the tomatoes.

2. Courgette half: In March, plant five shallots at 15cm intervals, sow chamomile and broadcast sow spinach. From the beginning of April, sow a row of leaf lettuce together with some radish, and by mid-April plant different types of lettuce, such as

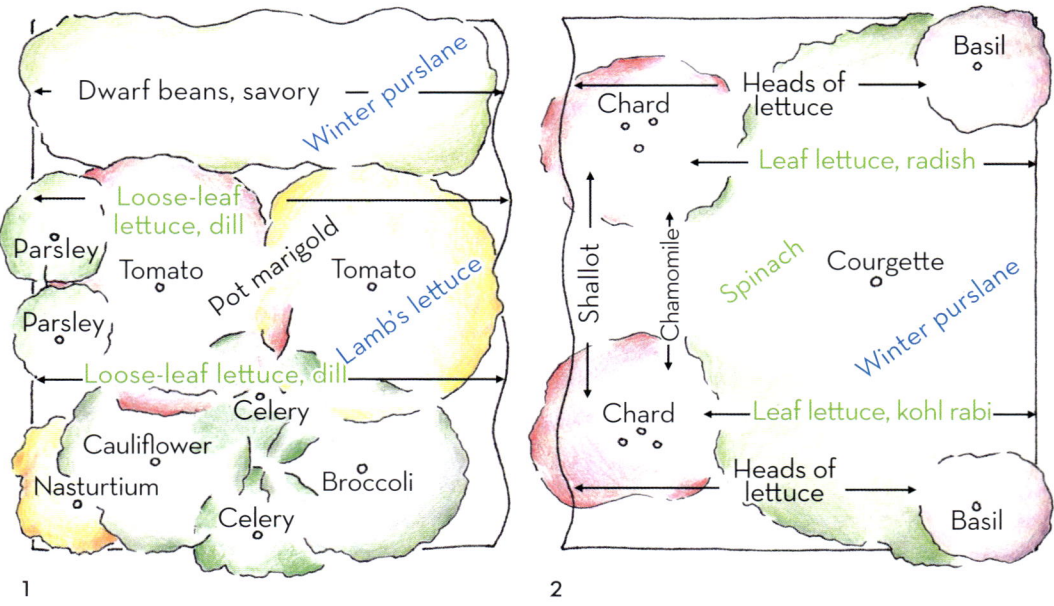

butterhead, iceberg, loose-leaf, cos, and cut and come again varieties. From mid-April, sow the second row of leaf lettuce, also including in that row two kohl rabi plants. Where the chard is to go, sow either two large seeds or up to five small ones, spaced slightly apart, and if the seedlings become too crowded thin them out. In mid-May, plant courgettes and basil, removing any spinach that is in the way. If gaps occur in the outer lettuce rows, plant endive and sugarloaf chicory if the courgettes allow enough room for these. In September you can broadcast sow winter purslane among the courgettes.

3. Cucumber half: In March, broadcast sow mustard where the peppers, cucumber and basil are to go, and then hoe it out in May. From the beginning of April, plant the onions at intervals of 5cm in the outer rows and also sow chervil and leaf chicory. In mid-May, plant two cucumber plants, two basil, two pepper and two marjoram plants. Sow dill with the basil. From August, sow radish, Abyssinian cabbage, rocket and lamb's lettuce in the onion rows, and broadcast sow orache among the cucumbers.

4. Quick vegetables: In March, plant the garlic at 10cm intervals. If it is warm enough you can also sow turnips and rocket. From April, sow early carrots, beetroot (with some coriander), peas beside a small trellis of twigs, some phacelia and three to five borage seeds. From mid-May, plant one or two small, single-flowered French marigolds and sow the summer purslane where you have harvested turnips and rocket. From July, once the early carrots and garlic have been harvested, sow Chinese mallow, and place the kohl rabi plants at 40cm intervals, with a summer lettuce planted between one kohl rabi and the next. In August, after you have harvested the peas and baby beets, sow spinach and plant endive and sugarloaf chicory. Finally, clear out the summer purslane in September and sow lamb's lettuce.

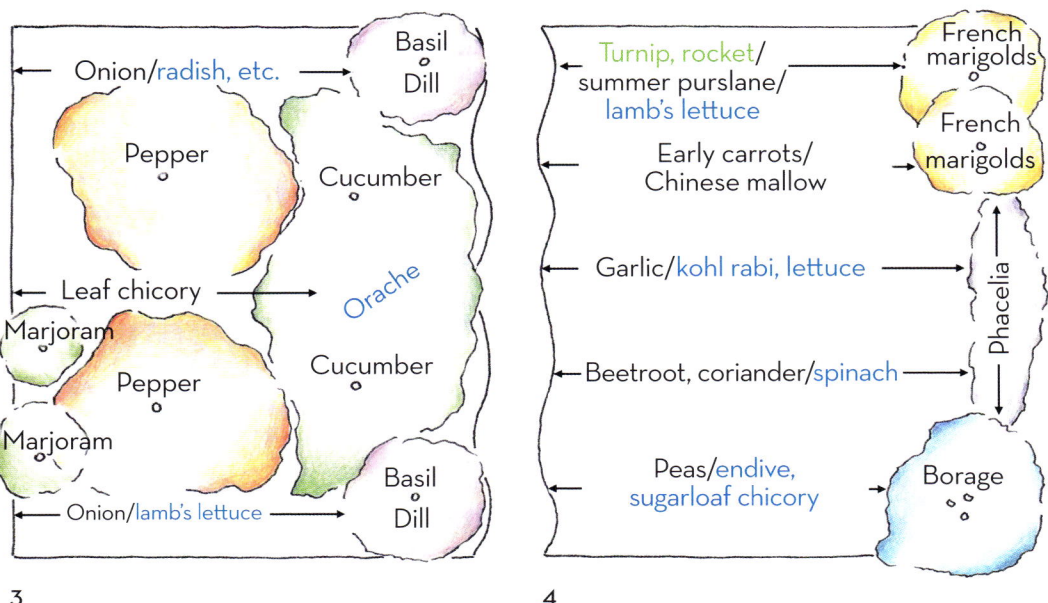

GOOD NEIGHBOURS UNDER THE TOMATO ROOF

It was once commonly believed that you could grow tomatoes in the same place every year. We now know that they produce a higher yield if they are grown on fresh soil.

In cool temperate countries, when tomatoes are grown outdoors they often suffer from leaf blight. As the fungal spores of leaf blight can only germinate on wet leaves, tomatoes are nearly always grown under cover to ensure that they are relatively protected from this fungal disease.

However, such 'tomato roofs' – in the form of a glasshouse or polytunnel – have a rigid structure under which tomatoes may be grown for decades in the same soil, producing lower yields each year as a result. One solution is to provide fresh growth medium each year by cultivating them in grow bags or large containers. Alternatively, if you prefer to grow them in the ground, you can improve tired soil by taking steps to encourage a wide variety of soil organisms and establish healthy, deep plant roots. In addition, if the foliage becomes too dense there will not be enough ventilation. As tomatoes need good air circulation to protect them from blight, the ideal solution is to have open roofs that are only pulled down on the west side, so that rain does not come in. Four ideas are suggested here that will allow you to reliably get high yields even under cover by growing them with good companions. Ring the changes fairly often, and never let the companions overcrowd the tomatoes.

1. BED In March, erect the tomato stakes at 60cm intervals, and broadcast sow pot marigolds in between them. Sow or plant a row of parsley (or carrots) 25cm in front of the stakes. From mid-May, plant the tomatoes in among the pot marigolds, and keep thinning out the latter so that they do not overcrowd the tomatoes. You could plant some French marigolds as well if you wish. In August/September, sow the marigold seeds again as green manure under the tomatoes.

2. BED From March, erect the tomato stakes at 1.2m intervals, and broadcast sow mustard. If you wish, sow a row of leaf lettuce approximately 15cm in front of or behind the stakes. From mid-May, hoe the mustard out where it is in the way, and plant the tomatoes. In the middle, between the tomato plants, sow some cucumber seeds in each gap. When planted outdoors and under airy tomato canopies, cucumbers and tomatoes together produce higher yields than they do in more cramped conditions in the greenhouse. In September, when the cucumbers are running out of energy, sow phacelia or orache.

3. BED In March, erect the tomato stakes at 60cm intervals, and sow a row of chamomile at a distance of 25cm behind the stakes. Sow a row of field beans at a distance of 10cm behind the stakes, and sow a row of spinach at a distance of 20cm in front of the stakes. If you wish, you could also plant some chives 25cm in front of the stakes. From mid-May, hoe out the broad beans and spinach and leave them lying as fertiliser, and then plant the tomatoes. Sow some low-growing nasturtiums along the former spinach row as they help to discourage slugs and snails. From early September, sow lamb's lettuce, rocket and leaf lettuce under the tomatoes.

4. BED In March, erect the tomato stakes at 60cm intervals, and broadcast sow white clover. Plant garlic at 15cm intervals in a row 25cm in front of the stakes, occasionally leaving a 30cm gap for basil. From mid-May, plant the tomatoes and basil. From November you can hoe out the white clover and leave it lying. Alternatively, you can leave it to grow until May, though the hoeing will then require more effort. Either way, the following year the tomatoes will benefit from this nitrogen fertiliser.

MODEL BEDS FOR THE ADVENTUROUS

A CONSTANT SUPPLY OF FRESH SALAD

Imagine being able to harvest green leaves outdoors all year round! Except during frost or snow, this can be achieved if you grow the right varieties at the right time. Over the winter you can harvest lots of winter greens, such as cress, winter purslane, tender kale leaves, Brussels sprouts, winter cress, cabbage, lamb's lettuce, spinach, chicory and chickweed.

Sowing

Sow lettuce every two to four weeks from March to September. In March, I sow lettuce in a cold frame and then re-plant it later. From mid-April I sow *in situ* where possible, as plants sown directly into the bed are more drought resistant and are not so prone to bolting, as they put down deeper roots. If there is still no room in the bed, I give priority to the lettuces in the seedbed or in other rows, and re-plant them in a rainy period.

Varieties and sowing times

Sowing times vary depending on the variety. With butterhead lettuce there are varieties suitable for early sowing outdoors. In cold conditions with low light levels they form beautiful heads, whereas in summer they would bolt without forming heads. In spring it is too cold and dark for the summer varieties, which need sun and warmth to form heads, but then do not bolt so easily. Frost-hardy winter varieties are sown in autumn so that they go into the winter with six to eight leaves – this enables them to withstand hard frosts and then continue to grow in the spring. There are also varieties suitable for growing at any time of year. These differences apply not just to butterhead lettuce, but also to different varieties of iceberg lettuce, endive, spinach, lamb's lettuce and radicchio. The relevant information can be found on the seed packets.

Winter-hardy varieties

Butterhead lettuce 'May King', 'May Wonder', 'Merveille des Quatre Saisons', 'Red Butterhead Maribor', 'Winter Butterhead', 'Wintermarie' and 'Bunter Kaufunger'

Spinach 'Andromeda', 'Matador', 'Monnopa', 'Nobel', 'Verdil' and 'Giant Winter'

Lamb's lettuce 'Dark Green Full Heart', 'Favor', 'Gala', 'Verte à Coeur Plein 2', 'Vit' and 'Volhart 3'

Young cos lettuce plants in the seedbed.

Radicchio and endive for the autumn harvest.

SOWING AND HARVESTING TIMES FOR SALAD VEGETABLES

Plant	Sowing	Harvest
Batavia lettuce	Mid-March until early August	Mid-May to mid-October
Buck's horn plantain	April to August	May to September
Butterhead lettuce (early varieties)	March to April	May to June
Butterhead lettuce (summer varieties)	April to June	June to September
Butterhead lettuce (winter varieties)	August to September	April/May
Chicory	Mid- to late May	November to January
Chinese cabbage	Mid-July	Late September to November
Chinese cabbage mixes	March/April and August/September	April/May and September to December
Chinese mallow	July	August to October
Cos lettuce	Mid-March to August	May to October
Endive (leaf)	Mid-March to late June	May to December
Endive (summer varieties)	June/July	August to October
Endive (winter varieties)	First two weeks of July	October to November
Iceberg lettuce (early varieties)	March to August	June to October
Iceberg lettuce (summer varieties)	May to late June	August to October
Lamb's lettuce (autumn varieties)	Late July to mid-August	September to October
Lamb's lettuce (early varieties)	March to April	April/May
Lamb's lettuce (winter varieties)	Mid-August to September	November to April
Leaf chicory	Early April to end of July	May to August
Leaf lettuce	March/April and September	April/May and October
Loose-leaf lettuce	March until early September	April to October
Oakleaf lettuce	March to August	May to October
Radicchio (autumn varieties)	Mid-June to mid-July	October to November
Radicchio (summer varieties)	Late May to mid-July	September
Radicchio (winter varieties)	Mid-July to early August	March to April
Rocket	March/April and August/September	April to June and September to December
Spinach (autumn varieties)	August/September	September/November
Spinach (early varieties)	March/April	April/May
Spinach (winter varieties)	September	October to March
Sugarloaf chicory	Mid-June until mid-July	September to December
Summer purslane	Mid-May to August	June to October

GREEN MANURE FOR PRE- OR POST-SOWING

For pre-sowing, green manures should be sown from March, and hoed down once they get in the way of the vegetables. Post-sowings can be done in the autumn after the vegetables.

What to do from spring through to winter
Apply compost before pre-sowing. The seeds will then germinate in the compost. As soon as you would like to sow vegetables, hoe down the pre-sowings together with any weeds growing alongside them, leave everything to dry out in the sun and then rake it slightly to one side. When rows become free from August onwards, post-sowings will still be growing abundantly. From mid-September until early October, sowing is still worthwhile, but the plants will remain small. Ideally, the green manure will be killed off by the frost over the winter, allowing you to pull the remains to one side in the spring and then sow in wonderfully crumbly soil. The plants listed in the table are highly suitable green manures for the vegetable garden.

Field beans If you hoe these out as a pre-sowing at a height of 30cm, the soft tissue of field beans will provide an ideal food source for soil organisms. This deep-rooting legume fixes nitrogen from the atmosphere with its root nodule bacteria, so makes a perfect pre-sowing green manure for tomatoes and other plants with high nutrient requirements, which are only sown or planted from mid-May.

Phacelia The most attractive of all green manures, this always fits into the crop rotation as it is not related to any vegetable. These tender plants are easy to hoe out and quick to rot down. If you sow phacelia up to August you will enjoy the enchanting fragrance of the flowers, which bees love. September sowings will not flower, but they do protect the soil.

White mustard This fast-growing plant forms a green carpet within two weeks. Before the vegetables are put in the ground, hoe out the 5–15cm tall mustard plants. The leaves are edible. When sown in the autumn, the plants will be killed off by frosts and then rot in the spring. Some varieties of white mustard help to suppress nematodes. They produce a substance that inhibits the development and reproduction of beet cyst eelworms, which feed on the roots of brassicas, beetroot and chard, causing the plants to grow poorly. White mustard is a brassica and can therefore transmit clubroot to other brassicas in a rotation, although the short-term interim cultivation of white mustard within the crop rotation does not usually have negative effects on other brassicas. However, it is important to hoe it out while it is still small, and white mustard should never be used in soils infected with clubroot.

Good partners Like French marigolds, the lyme grass variety 'Pratex' helps to suppress the number of free-living pratylenchus nematodes, but only to a limited extent. However, lyme grass does grow more vigorously than the French marigold, which is a magnet for slugs and snails. It is also very good at suppressing weeds, and it always fits into the crop rotation. If you are using lyme grass alone, sow at a density of 12g seed/m^2. Lyme grass mixed with phacelia looks wonderful.

Crimson clover (left) fixes nitrogen; lyme grass (right) suppresses nematodes.

QUANTITIES AND TIMING OF SOWING OF GREEN MANURES

Plants	Sowing quantity per m²	Sowing time as a pre-sowing	Sowing time as a post-sowing	Frost tender in winter
Buckwheat	10g	-	Until late Aug	Yes
Common vetch	10g	From March	Aug	Yes
Crimson clover	3g	From March	-	No
Egyptian clover	5g	From March	Early Aug	Yes
Field beans	40 seeds	From mid-Feb	Aug	Yes
Lyme grass	12g	-	From mid-July until late Aug	Yes
Oil radish	4g	-	Until mid-Sept	From –11 °C
Persian clover	3g	From March	Until mid-Aug	Yes
Phacelia	1–4g	April	Until mid-Sept	From –8 °C
Ramtil	1g	-	Until mid-Aug	Yes
White mustard	2–5g	From March	Until late Sept	From –7 °C

Eight sample beds for the adventurous

The following pages outline useful yet unconventional vegetable beds and cultivation. In all cases the yield more than compensates for the work involved.

Ideas for cardboard

Annually covering the ground with cardboard and grass cuttings saves you from having to do a lot of weeding under soft fruit and ornamental shrubs or over the summer between larger perennials.

In their size and arrangement these beds are similar to the template beds for beginners. Here, too, the crop rotation will be correct if you create the beds in the order described. For those without a vegetable bed, you may first need to convert a lawn or a neglected bed into a fertile growing space.

A NEW BED WITH LITTLE EFFORT

In autumn or very early spring, mow over the lawn area. If the soil underneath is suitable for vegetables and rich in nutrients (reliable indicators of this include dandelions, stinging nettles, cleavers or chickweed), put down one or two layers of

1

cardboard (large cardboard boxes can be opened out and the packaging tape removed). Place the pieces of cardboard tightly together so that not a single leaf can get through. On top of them place a few heavy stones, some compost, grass cuttings, leaves and any other material that will rot down well and conceal the cardboard (otherwise blackbirds in their search for earthworms may shred it). From mid- to late May, when everything under the cardboard has turned yellow, dig holes in the cardboard layer and place potatoes in them (with spacings of 30 × 75cm). The potato plants will provide shade for the area during the summer, so that the soil organisms can thrive. After the potatoes have been harvested, sow phacelia and lyme grass.

KEEP WEEDS IN THE DARK

If the ground is completely congested with elder, couch grass, horsetail, creeping thistle or blackberry roots, use cardboard to totally exclude light for another year, and in the absence of even a glimpse of daylight the underground rhizomes will eventually rot. After that you can plant the potatoes.

BREAKING UP COMPACTED AREAS

If the ground is compacted (reliable indicators of this include broadleaf plantain, knotweed, creeping buttercup, horsetail or creeping thistle), loosen it up with a garden fork, digging in as deep as the fork will go. Then add a 3–5cm thick layer of compost and cover it with the cardboard and thick mulch. If the compaction is not too severe, potatoes and green manure can successfully be grown after this. To break up heavily compacted ground, after harvesting the potatoes sow a green manure of field beans, oil radish and lupins. This will not fit into the crop rotation before the Native American bed (see page 66). For this reason it is best to instead start with Bed 5 (see page 74), but to replace the cauliflower with celeriac. If the ground is still compacted and the vegetables are not growing, try using a deep loosening green manure for another year. Sunflowers, flax, alfalfa and Chinese mallow are all suitable for this. If this is not effective, a raised bed can be constructed, which is quite labour-intensive to create, but thereafter will be really easy to work.

1. Where the vegetable bed is due to be made, cover the grass with cardboard so that the plants underneath it die off.

2. Compost contains soil organisms, which give the soil a crumbly texture.

3. Straw decomposes very slowly but ensures that plenty of air is present for soil organisms.

NATIVE AMERICAN BED

PLANTS IN THE BED

Basil
Courgettes
Green manure
Phacelia
Runner beans
Squash
Sweetcorn

With squashes, sweetcorn and beans, this is the traditional Native American bed. If you move the crops 60cm further on within the bed, you can leave it in the same place for two years.

WHAT TO DO WHEN

March/April If green manure from the previous year germinates, allow it to grow. If not, sow fresh green manure (see page 63).

May In the first week of May, hoe a 60cm-wide strip in the middle of the bed, let the plants dry out and then pull them aside. Allow the rest of the green manure to continue to grow until it gets in the way. About three days later sow the sweetcorn in the middle of the bed in clumps of four seeds, with the seeds spaced 20cm apart and the groupings spaced 120cm apart. To ensure that four strong plants will grow in each clump, sow extra seeds and thin out the weaker seedlings. When the sweetcorn is 20cm tall, sow six runner bean seeds around the sweetcorn clump at a distance of 15cm, and allow four of the seedlings to grow. A wide variety of squash plants can now also be grown between the sweetcorn clumps. For the cucumbers, sow two to three groups of two seeds each in one space between the sweetcorn

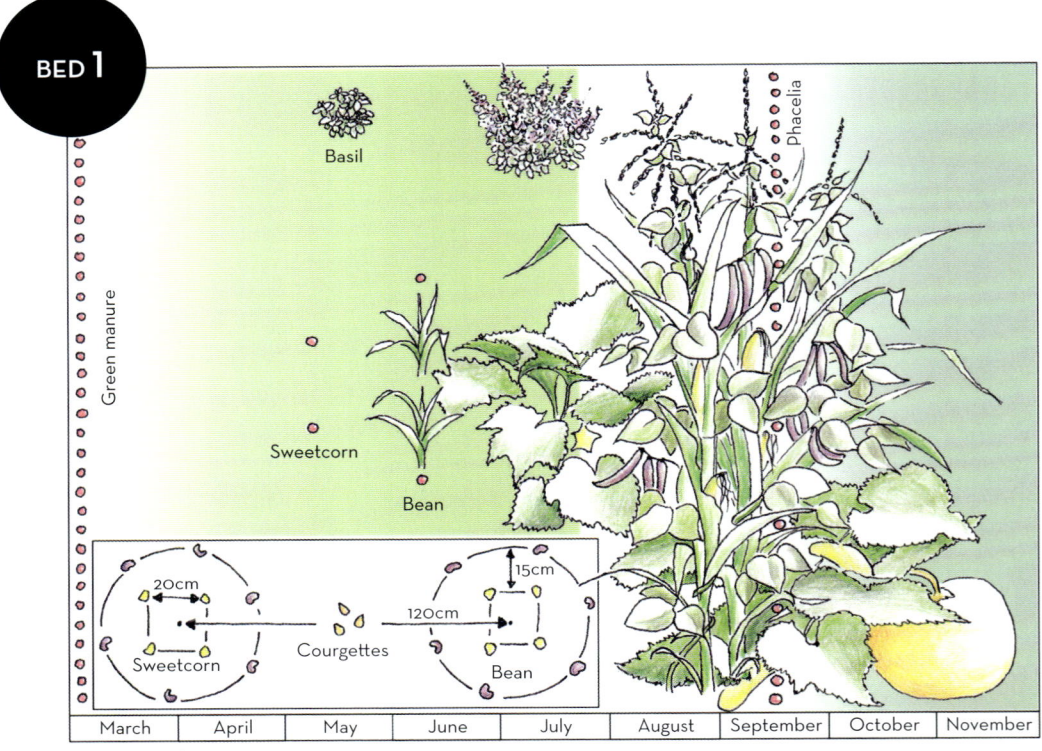

BED 1

clumps; for the courgettes sow one group of three seeds, and for the squash plants leave two to three spaces between the sweetcorn clumps, depending on the squash variety. At the edge plant some basil. If you bring on the sweetcorn indoors and plant it out in mid-May, the whole bed will mature slightly earlier.

July/August Harvest the beans every two to three days. The sweetcorn is ready to harvest as soon as the silks have dried at the top of the corn cob. The kernels will then still be tender and milky on the inside, with the best flavour.

September As soon as you have cleared away the first plants, sow phacelia into the empty gaps.

GOOD PARTNERS

Trials from across the world prove that sweetcorn and legumes produce much higher yields when grown together than as single crops. This applies to peas, field beans, dwarf beans and runner beans. If you want runner beans to twine around sweetcorn you must choose suitable varieties, sowing and harvest times, and plant spacings so that the beans do not overcrowd the sweetcorn and reduce its yields. Cucumbers, courgettes and squashes shade the ground. When grown together with sweetcorn and legumes, they also produce higher yields.

Runner beans For growing up and around sweetcorn, the head-high climbing bean varieties such as 'Trail of Tears' or 'Yellow Climbing Bean' are suitable. Runner beans that do not climb so high, such as 'Neckar Gold', 'Neckar Queen' and 'Blauhilde', also

'Uchiki Kuri', Bantam sweetcorn and 'Blauhilde' in the Native American bed.

work well. If they grow too tall, cut them back and they will then develop side shoots lower down. I particularly like 'Blauhilde', as the slugs and snails leave it alone. Scarlet runner beans grow too vigorously where I live, so I prefer to sow them on a sturdy frame.

Sweetcorn varieties For the Native American bed, use tall, sturdy varieties. The robust variety 'Golden Bantam', which grows 2m tall and has sweet cobs that ripen over several days, is particularly suitable. The three extra-sweet varieties – 'Damaun', 'Mezdi' and 'Tramunt' – grow 1.8m tall and ripen one after the other as soon as 'Golden Bantam' has been harvested. If you like decorative cobs, grow 'Rainbow Inca', 'Oaxacan Green' or 'Bloody Butcher', all tall-growing varieties that taste sweet when unripe and become colourful when allowed to fully ripen.

Squashes All varieties are suitable. The vigorous varieties need growing space next to the bed as well (so that they can grow out onto the grass or through robust vegetables). The orange-coloured Hokkaido 'Uchiki Kuri' is my favourite.

My favourite Hokkaido squash – 'Uchiki Kuri'.

PEAS-CARROT-BRASSICA-HORSERADISH BED

PLANTS IN THE BED

Chervil
Chinese cabbage
Chinese mallow
Early carrots
Florence fennel
Garlic
Horseradish
Kale
Leaf and loose-leaf lettuces
Pak choi
Radishes
Rocket
Sugarsnap peas
Turnips

Here there is plenty of scope for juggling with different types of vegetables, as the crop rotation is very flexible. In mid-summer there is a shift change on this bed!

WHAT TO DO WHEN

Early April Sow a row of sugarsnap peas 20cm away from the edge, and a row of rocket 35cm further on. If you do not need a whole row of rocket, divide the row and also sow turnips, radishes and horseradish. Due to problems with cabbage stem flea beetle, I sow leaf or loose-leaf lettuces in between, and chervil to keep away slugs and snails. At a distance of 15cm from the other edge, plant garlic cloves at 30cm intervals and sow an early carrot variety in between them. I scatter tansy powder over the seeds (see page 73). At a distance of 25cm further, plant a row of lettuces, dividing the row so that you can sow different varieties. Do try a 'Misticanza' mix with the slightly salty-tasting buck's horn plantain, or heritage lettuce varieties such as 'Hart's Tongue' or 'Speckled Trout'.

July The whole of the bed can now be gradually harvested. On the pea side, apply a 2cm-thick layer of compost, and 25cm from the edge plant one part of the row with kale and the other part with Chinese cabbage, both at spacings of 40cm. If the kale plants are placed at 60cm intervals there will still be room for lettuces in between. Then 45cm further in plant Florence fennel at 30cm intervals, and in one part of the row you can sow Chinese mallow. About 15cm from the other edge, sow winter radishes and scatter some tansy powder to protect against cabbage fly. From mid-July until early August you can also sow pak choi in one part of the row, or from August you can sow the large daikon radishes.

October Apart from the kale, everything should be harvested before the first hard frost is forecast.

GOOD PARTNERS

In trials, when lettuce, rocket, peas and carrots were grown together they produced increased yields. The lettuces keep cabbage stem flea beetle away from the brassicas. The small brassicas grow well with the peas and

Buck's horn plantain

MODEL BEDS FOR THE ADVENTUROUS

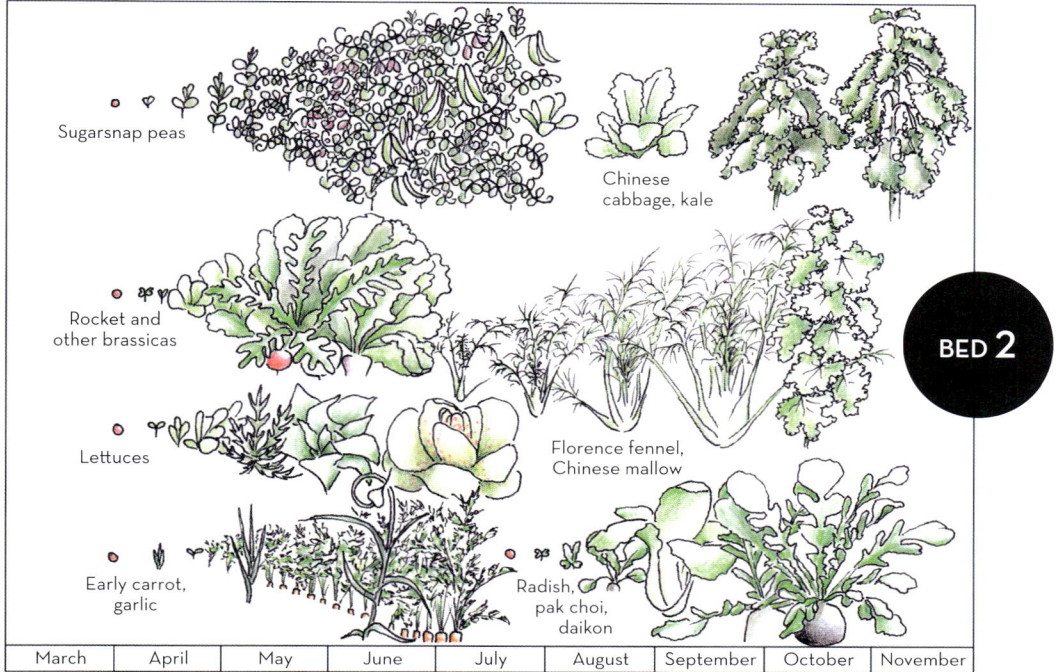

are ready to harvest before the latter spread out. The nitrogen fixed by the pea root nodules later benefits the nutrient-hungry brassicas. Garlic deters carrot fly, and when grown together with peas and lettuce has been found to produce higher yields than when grown alone.

Chinese cabbage In order to grow rapidly this needs deep, humus-rich soil and sufficient nutrients and water. Young plants are best grown in pots, as Chinese cabbage does not tolerate transplanting well. Some attractive heritage varieties can only be sown from mid-July.

Chinese mallow This grows without a problem and likes to self-seed. I often add the young leaves to salads, as they are both tasty and very good for the digestive system.

Rocket Late sowings in August do best, as they do not flower and can be grown as a cut and come again crop until the first hard frosts. Well-watered rocket has a more tender, mild flavour.

Pak choi This resembles chard but tastes like Chinese cabbage. It is sown in the second half of July and harvested seven to nine weeks later.

Chervil If hot weather causes this plant to bolt and flower too quickly, the flowers also taste good.

Winter radish If you do not like the robust, pungent flavour of black winter radishes, try daikon radishes. These large, white root vegetables originating from Japan are deliciously mild. Many other radish varieties are also suitable for sowing in July and August.

Daikon radish

YACON BED

PLANTS IN THE BED

Beetroot
Borage
Broad beans
Kohl rabi
Leaf and loose-leaf lettuces
Orache
Tree spinach
Yacons

Kohl rabi and lettuces grow next to the yacons, and are harvested when the yacons need more space.

This is one of the beds that require hardly any work over the summer. However, you do need a cool dry cellar or shed for the yacon plants to overwinter in.

WHAT TO DO WHEN

March Pull the mulch to one side and harvest the kale soon. About 15cm from the edge, sow colourful orache in one-third of the row. Then, 25cm away from the other edge, sow early broad beans 80cm apart. Between the two rows spread a layer of compost 2cm thick, broadcast sow white mustard (the green area in the illustration) and sprinkle fine mulch lightly over everything to prevent the compost from drying out.

April In the rest of the orache row, sow tree spinach as well as leaf and loose-leaf lettuces. In the broad bean row, plant an early kohl rabi variety between two broad bean plants. In the gaps between the kohl rabi and the broad beans, sow either two borage seeds or five or six beetroot seeds at 4cm intervals.

Mid-May Hoe out the mustard as well as any weeds that are growing alongside, allow this material to dry out, then pull it slightly to the side and fetch the yacon plants. Plant them at 60cm intervals in the middle of the bed. The first, tender orache leaves will now be ready to cut. Mulch the whole bed, but especially the yacons.

June/July Harvest the broad beans, orache, tree spinach, borage and kohl rabi when the plants become overcrowded. We pick the beetroot when the diameter measures 4cm.

October/November When the upper leaves of the yacons have been blackened by frost, cut the stalks off and dig the tubers out of the ground. Harvest the large, lengthy tubers into crates so that you can prepare them in the kitchen. The small, knobbly tubers on the stalks can be covered with some earth or sand and then stored in a cool dry place such as a cellar or shed over winter.

GOOD PARTNERS

In my experience, orache, tree spinach, kohl rabi, beetroot, lettuces, borage and broad beans make good companion plants. Rocket also grows very well next to yacons.

Orache This is available in green, yellow, red and purple forms. It looks wonderful if you have them

MODEL BEDS FOR THE ADVENTUROUS

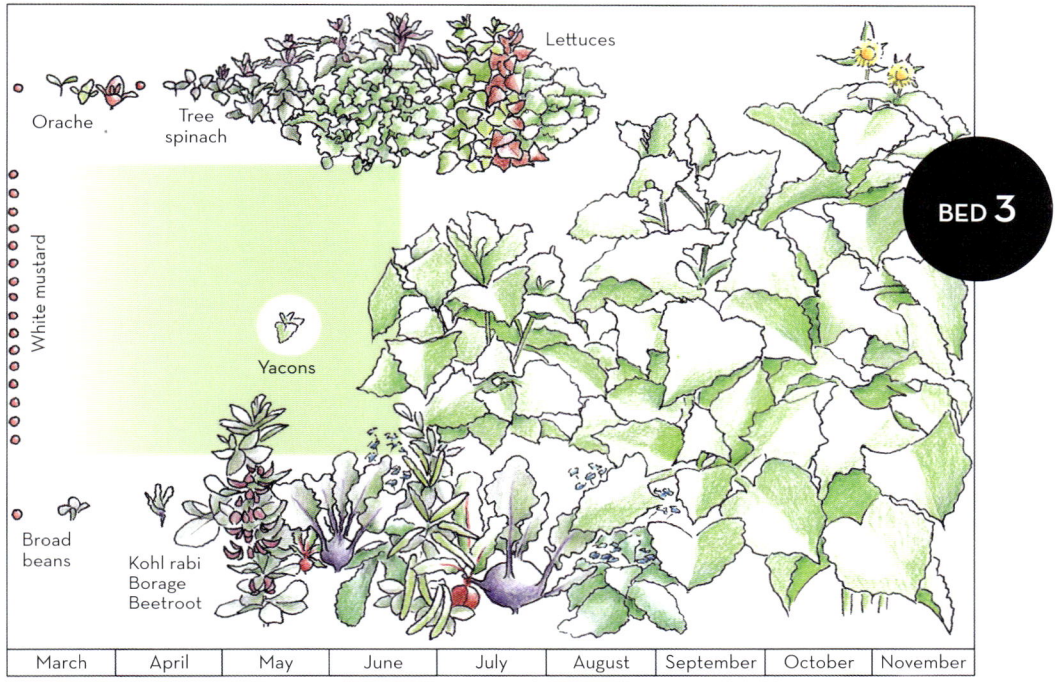

all, but the green one grows best. The thick young leaves go well with spinach and lettuces. Cut-back plants seem to almost always sprout again. However, once they start to flower the leaves lose their flavour, and the plants (which are by now head-high) then produce thousands of seeds.

Tree spinach Harvest and treat the plants just like orache. If you allow orache and tree spinach (giant goosefoot) to self-seed you will later find seedlings all over the garden. However, their violet centres make tree spinach seedlings easy to identify.

Yacons The large dahlia-like tubers of yacon are soft and taste sweet like fruit. We eat them peeled as crudités together with carrots and almonds before meals, or slice them into fruit salads. Children love them.

Leaf and loose-leaf lettuces Sow leaf lettuces close together and cut them off at a height of 2–3cm when they are approximately 12cm tall. They will then sprout again two or three more times. Sow the lettuces further apart, and pluck off the outer leaves. You can also plant them singly, spaced 20–30cm apart, and allow them to grow into open heads, which you then harvest as a head of lettuce.

Borage The blue flowers of borage never fail to delight me and they taste great. Once the plants are established, ants carry the large seeds everywhere, so you only have to intervene when weeding to control where they grow.

Borage

Orache

Tree spinach

POTATO BED AS RECOMMENDED BY MARGARETE LANGERHORST

PLANTS IN THE BED

Field beans
Phacelia
Potatoes
White mustard

The idea of cultivating potatoes without earthing up but instead using a lot of mulch originated in the United States, was developed further in Austria and has proved to be a great success.

WHAT TO DO WHEN

March Sow a row of field beans 10cm from the edges and in the centre, and broadcast sow white mustard in between. At the end of March, chit the potatoes in shallow trays out of direct sunlight at 12–15°C.

May At the beginning of May, hoe the mustard out, allow it to dry and then pull it up towards the field beans. After a week or so, mark out the potato rows at a distance of 30cm from the edges, and make a hole about 10cm deep at 40cm intervals. Meanwhile, allow the potatoes to soak in herbal horsetail tea for 30 minutes. Then roll them in rock flour, lay them in the holes and cover them with soil. Sprinkle the ground between the field beans with a 2cm layer of compost, and then lay old plant stems, followed by grass cuttings, rock flour and slightly dried grass cuttings on top. The total thickness may now be 15–25cm, but the layers will later break down and collapse. Finally, pour the remains of the horsetail tea on top. Cut

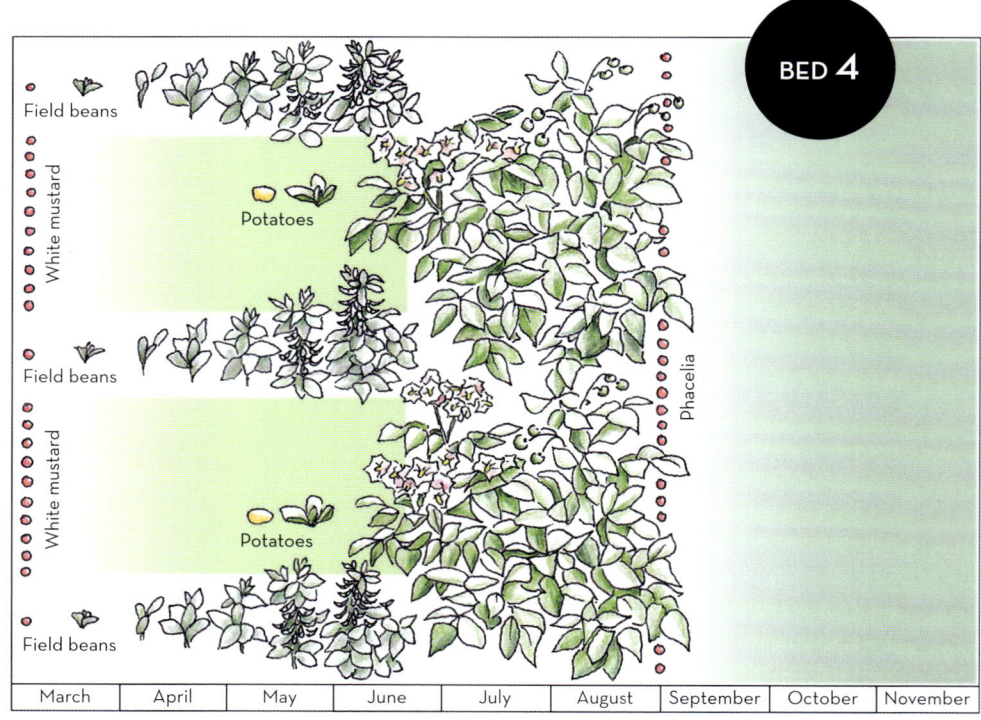

BED 4

1. Tansy repels many insect pests.
2. In June, Bed 4 is freshly mulched and the field beans are already rotting.

the field beans down as soon as they flower, and leave them on the ground as mulch.

July As a preventative measure to protect against late blight, spray the potatoes with horsetail tea or onion skin slurry every 14 days.

August/September When the potato leaves and stems have died back completely, harvest the potatoes a few days later in dry weather. Then level the soil a little, distribute the mulch and the potato foliage evenly and sow phacelia, shaking the seeds into the mulch with the rake. Place a very thin layer of grass cuttings on top to keep the moisture in.

GOOD PARTNERS

The mustard keeps the soil really moist and crumbly. The field beans fix atmospheric nitrogen, which later benefits the potatoes when the beans rot down. Potato plants topple over easily, burying all the neighbouring vegetables underneath them, which is why I prefer not to distribute them over all the vegetable beds. Instead, I group them together next to robust vegetables such as yacons, where they cannot do much damage. The phacelia keeps the soil loose after the potato harvest and brings up nutrients that would otherwise be washed out over the winter.

Tansy This robust perennial does not get on well with vegetables, so it is located in the wild part of my flower garden. The strong fragrance of the tansy drives away pests, and it is an important nectar plant for bees, butterflies and moths.

Tansy powder

Dry the leaves and flowers, grind them and sprinkle the powder to deter pests like carrot fly. Tansy tea and tansy broth are also effective.

SHALLOT-CARROT-BLACK SALSIFY-CHICORY BED

PLANTS IN THE BED

Black cumin
Black salsify
Chicory
Dill
Late carrots
Leaf chicory
Salsify
Shallots
Winter lettuces

Black salsify

Salsify

There are many delicious vegetables in this bed, but black salsify, chicory and shallots also involve a lot of work, so feel free to simplify the plan if you wish.

WHAT TO DO WHEN

March Pull the mulch from the ground and hoe the entire bed to a depth of 1cm so that the weed seeds germinate and the soil warms up.
Early April Plant shallots at 15cm intervals in rows 15cm and 45cm from the edge. Then, 15cm from the other side, divide the chicory row into four and sow the black salsify in the first quarter and the salsify in the second quarter of the row.
Mid-April Sow the leaf chicory in the third quarter of the chicory row. Then, 45cm away from the edge, sow late carrots, and at 12cm intervals allow one dill or black cumin seed to fall into the row at the same time.
Mid-May Sow chicory in the fourth quarter of the chicory row.
August When the shallot foliage has almost died back, pull the shallots out of the soil and leave them to dry outside in the sun for a few days. Then store them in a cool dry cellar or shed. In mid-August, broadcast sow the winter lettuce (about one seed every 5cm) over the shallot rows.
October/November Before the first hard frost, cover the carrots with moist sand in a cool dry cellar or shed, and pot the chicory. The winter-hardy black and ordinary salsify can be harvested until March, but be aware that mice also like them. The leaf chicory will produce fresh leaves in spring until it flowers. The winter lettuce will continue to grow in spring.
January Fetch the large chicory pots from the cellar or shed, and place them in a dark place to sprout.

GOOD PARTNERS

Black salsify and shallots repel carrot fly, and carrots keep onion fly at bay. Nothing is grown between the shallots as they need plenty of light and air. Trials have shown that carrots and lettuces, when grown together, produce higher yields. Dill promotes the germination of carrots.
Black salsify The soil must be both deep and loose so that the roots grow straight down, as peeling branched roots is a very fiddly job. If mice are not a problem, harvest the roots and use them fresh, as roots damaged during harvesting do not keep well. That said, it is not easy to get the long roots out of the ground undamaged.
Salsify Related to black salsify, not quite as tasty, but much more robust in cultivation, salsify often produces abundant yields. You can harvest it fresh throughout the winter and do not have to peel it. In spring the bleached shoots taste wonderful. To bleach them, earth up the plants a little and harvest the fresh shoots from the soil. In the second year the plants flower and the roots become tough.

Shallots Although they are smaller than onions, shallots are sweeter and more aromatic. In late March or early April break them apart and plant the largest ones so that that the top is sticking out of the ground. If you want to harvest large shallots, break off some of the daughter bulbs in May, and the remaining ones will then thicken up. Shallots are great for storing.

Leaf chicory This is very useful as it produces slightly bitter salad leaves all year round. You can pick the tender leaves constantly, but don't remove the heart leaves. New leaves will sprout in spring, and later the plants will flower and readily set seed.

Chicory When harvesting, cut the leaves back to a length of 2cm. Immediately after harvesting, I pot the roots relatively close together in large pots of moist garden soil and then place them in a cool but frost-free place (0–1°C). In January I move the pots into a cool hallway (12–18°C), water them, and place a pot of the same size upside down over the top to exclude light. When I have cut the first chicons after four to six weeks, I can expect to have a second harvest or even a third one.

Black cumin This is easy to grow and is not related to any vegetable, so it always fits into the crop rotation. The capsules ripen in September and are easy to open.

Alliums and leaf chicory like each other.

BED 5

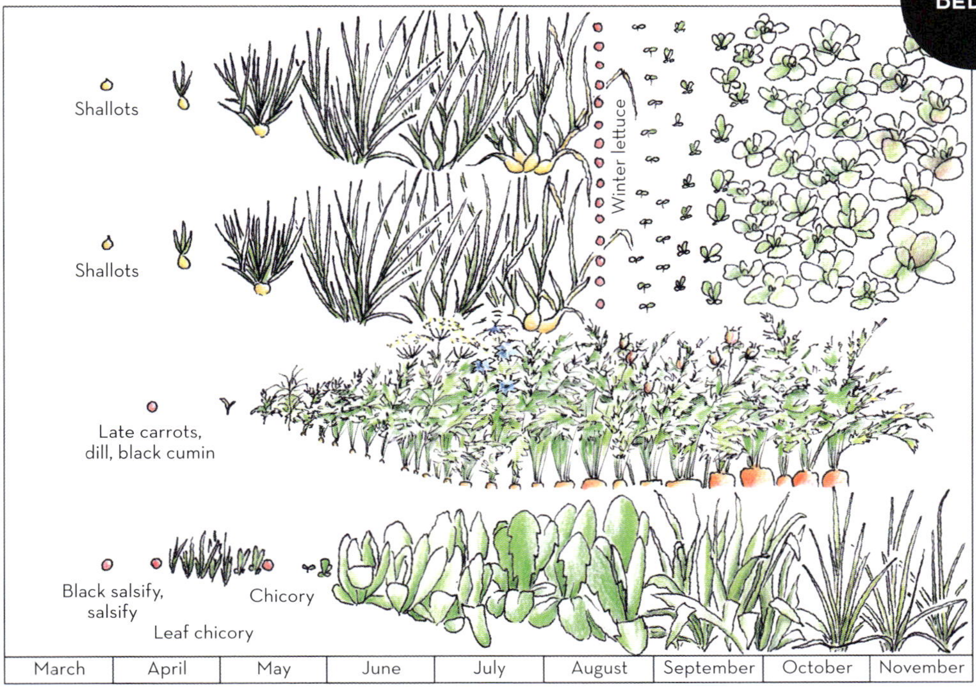

Shallots

Shallots

Winter lettuce

Late carrots, dill, black cumin

Black salsify, salsify

Chicory

Leaf chicory

| March | April | May | June | July | August | September | October | November |

CELERY-CAULIFLOWER-LEEK-PARSNIP BED

PLANTS IN THE BED

Cauliflower
Celeriac
Celery
Florence fennel
Palm kale
Parsnips
Red cabbage
Romanesco
Root parsley
Spinach
Winter leeks
Winter lettuces

Palm kale tastes heavenly with garlic and feta.

This is a variation of my favourite celery–leek–celery bed. Although it involves a lot of variety, it can easily be simplified.

WHAT TO DO WHEN

March Mark out two rows 20cm and 40cm away from the edge. Sow parsnips in the outer row, where they have already been harvested, and sow spinach in the inner row.

April When harvesting the lettuce, space the winter lettuce (see page 60) at 20–30cm intervals. We also eat a lot of salsify and black salsify at this time! Wherever space becomes available in the marked parsnip row, until mid-April sow either more parsnips or root parsley. You can harvest leaf chicory on a continual basis (see Bed 5).

Mid-May If you have not already done so, now completely clear away all last year's chicory. Plant up the remainder of the marked parsnip row with Florence fennel and celery, spacing the plants 30cm apart. The winter lettuce harvest is now gradually coming to an end, so 25cm from the edge you can mark up the celeriac–cabbage row. Place the celeriac plants 80cm apart, with cauliflower, romanesco, palm kale or red cabbage planted between them, depending on your requirements. In a row 55cm away from the parsnip side, plant winter leeks at 20cm intervals.

August Where cauliflower or romanesco are ripening, from the end of August sow Siberian kale or radishes in the gaps that appear (not shown on the plan).

October/November Harvest celeriac, palm kale, red cabbage, radishes, fennel and celery before the first hard frosts. Siberian kale, leek, parsnip and root parsley can remain *in situ* for harvesting in winter. However, voles are extremely fond of parsnips, so you may want to plant something else if your garden attracts voles!

GOOD PARTNERS

Celeriac and cauliflower are very good companions, growing better together than on their own. The celeriac is an excellent deterrent for cabbage whitefly. If you have problems with the small cabbage whitefly, sow some white clover in the cauliflower row in March so that the base of each cauliflower has plenty growing around it. Leeks keep carrot fly away from the parsnips, and because leek roots are shallow whereas parsnips have deep roots, they grow well together.

Cauliflower/romanesco Both of these vegetables need an optimal, even supply of nutrients and water. When it is warm, cauliflower only forms leaves – it requires several cool days in order to flower.

Palm kale From July until the first hard frost, harvest the tender young leaves, but leave the heart in place to grow on. The leaves taste like a tender version of kale.

MODEL BEDS FOR THE ADVENTUROUS

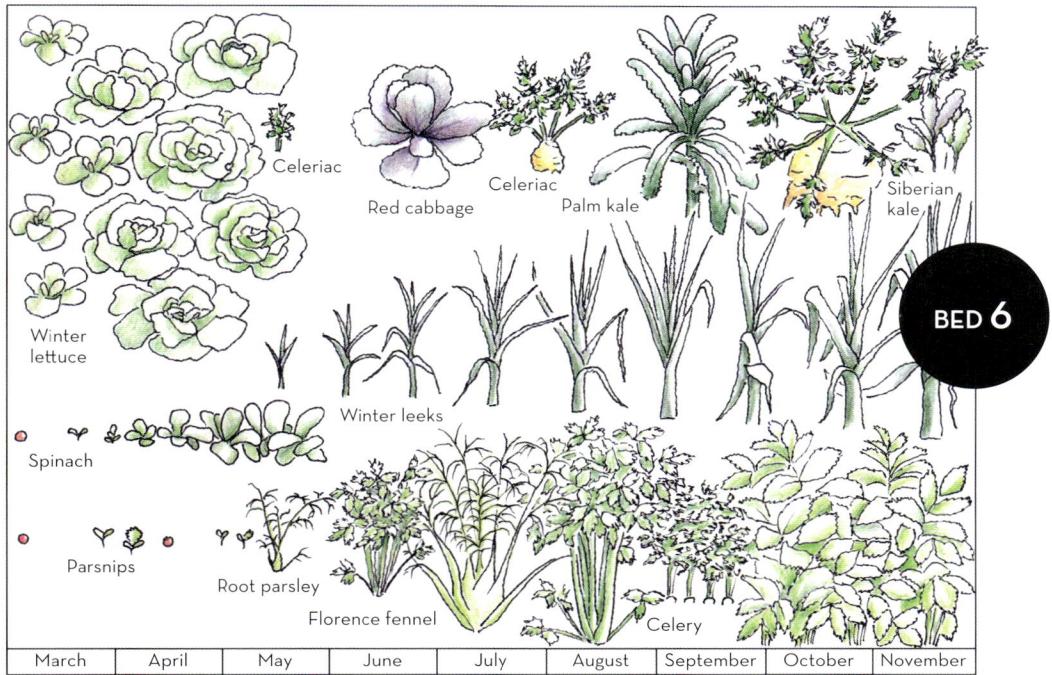

Celery The new, green-stemmed varieties no longer have to be planted deep in order for them to remain tender, nor is it necessary to wrap them up and bleach them. As a result, celery is now easier to grow. From August into the winter I cut individual stems and leaves as a seasoning for stews and salads.

Siberian kale This relatively frost-hardy, robust leaf cabbage tastes mildly of kohl rabi. Harvest the leaves when they are 5–7cm long. In spring the harvest continues until April.

Parsnips The robust, creamy-white roots grow easily, and taste best when harvested fresh from the ground in winter. The seeds can only be kept for one year.

Root parsley Although this is less common in the UK, the creamy parsnip-like taste is delicious. Crop rotation is particularly important due to root fungi. Substitute parsnips for root parsley if it is unavailable.

Florence fennel One of the new bolt-resistant varieties (e.g. 'Zefa Fino') is recommended here, which can be sown in spring. If you are only going to sow in the first half of July (see page 68), the older varieties are also suitable.

Celeriac, winter leeks and cauliflower grow very well together.

BABY BEET-KOHL RABI-BEAN BED

PLANTS IN THE BED

Autumn turnip
Baby beets
Dwarf beans
Kohl rabi
Loose-leaf lettuce
Radicchio
Savory
Siberian kale
Spinach
Swedes
Winter endive
Winter purslane

Lettuce and kohl rabi grow really well together.

You can make this bed even more productive over winter by opting for radicchio and autumn turnips for overwintering, as these are suitable for mild winters caused by climate change.

WHAT TO DO WHEN

March Harvest Siberian kale on a continual basis (see Bed 6). On the other side of the bed, sow a row of spinach 15cm and 30cm away from the edge of the bed, or grow parsnips and celery.

Mid-April Sow beetroot 15cm away from the edge, using closer spacing (4cm apart) for baby beets. Then, 35cm and 75cm from the edge, plant a row of loose-leaf lettuces spaced 30cm apart. A giant variety of kohl rabi (for example, 'Superschmelz') can be planted or sown in the same row, between the loose-leaf lettuces. The Siberian kale from Bed 6 can gradually be removed.

Mid-May Harvest the spinach so that you can sow the early dwarf beans and savory 20cm from the edge.

July The baby beets are now ready to harvest, so you can sow radicchio or winter endive in the row from early to mid-July.

August Where the dwarf beans have been harvested at the beginning of August you can plant turnips at intervals of 50cm. Where you want the beans to remain in place for a little longer, you could sow autumn turnips in mid-August. Alternatively, of course, you can simply leave the beans *in situ* and wait for a second harvest.

Mid-September Harvest the kohl rabi as needed and broadcast sow winter purslane under the kohl rabi plants.

October/November Before the first hard frosts, everything except for the winter purslane and possibly hardy autumn turnips or radicchio varieties should be cleared from the bed.

GOOD PARTNERS

Kohl rabi and lettuce make a good team, as the kohl rabi grows tall and provides the lettuce with shade from the sun, while the lettuce shades the exposed root area of the kohl rabi and drives away the cabbage stem flea beetle. Savory repels bean aphids. In trials, when grown together with dwarf beans, kohl rabi and beetroot produced higher yields than when they were grown on their own.

Kohl rabi Here one of the giant varieties such as 'Superschmelz' is being grown. The bulbs grow big but rarely become woody. Harvest from July until November. These bulbs store well. In the rest of the bed plans shown, 'normal'-sized kohl rabi varieties are being grown. These are ready to harvest 6–12 weeks after planting, and then quickly become woody.

Radicchio Growing here is 'Palla Rossa', an autumn variety that only tolerates light frosts. From mid-July sow 'Rossa di Verona', a red variety that can overwinter in mild winters with some protection, and is ready to harvest from February through to

April. There are also varieties suitable for growing in spring.

Winter endive This grows best when sown directly in the open ground in the first half of July, as its tap root will then reach a depth of about 1.5m in the soil, whereas the roots of planted endive often only reach a depth of 35cm. As the leaves suffer frost damage at -6°C, either consume them all by November or cover the plants with leaves.

Swedes A tasty yellow variety such as 'Wilhelmsburger' – harvested when it is 10–12cm in diameter – is a real delicacy. In contrast, the large, white cattle fodder beets have a bland flavour long associated in people's minds with wartime cooking. Swedes can withstand temperatures down to around -6°C. If it gets colder than that, cover them with leaves or soil.

Autumn turnips Turnips grow quickly and taste delicious if harvested when they are small and tender. Many varieties are frost-hardy, but after being frozen they no longer taste as good.

1. Radicchio 'Palla Rossa'
2. For the 4cm baby beets, sow the beetroot closer together than usual.

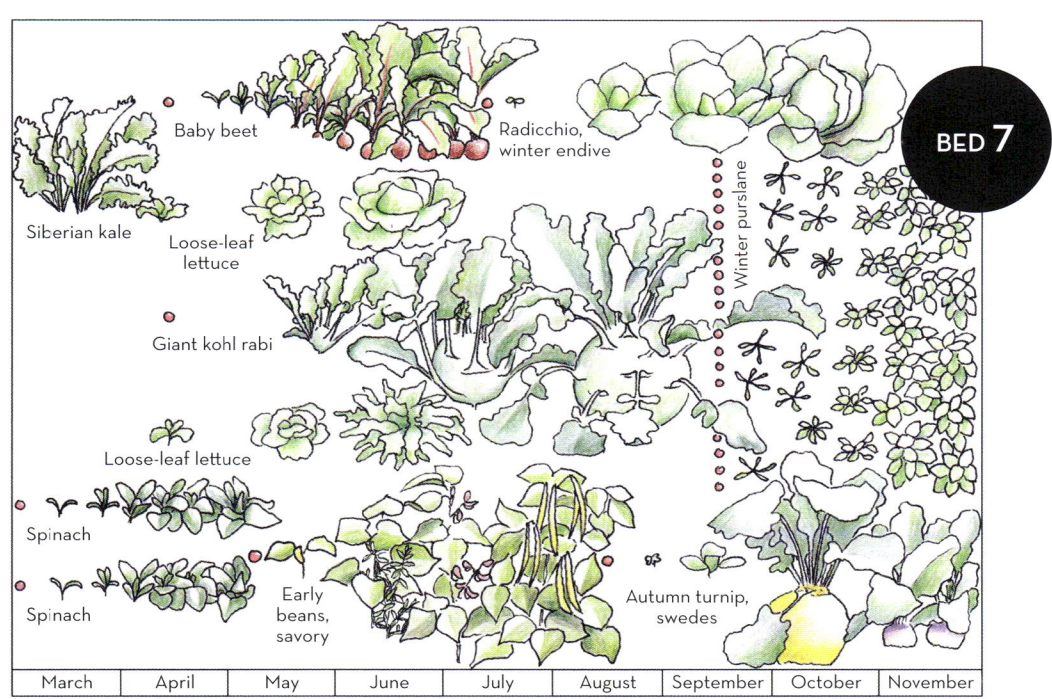

BED 7

COLOURFUL TOMATO BED

PLANTS IN THE BED

Basil
Borage
Chard
Cucumbers
Dill
Garlic
Nasturtiums
New Zealand spinach
Parsley
Pot marigolds
Staked tomatoes
Winter purslane
Winter rye

This bed is a feast for both the eyes and the palate. Take prompt action if the cucumbers or tomatoes start to become crowded, as both require plenty of circulating air around them.

WHAT TO DO WHEN

April In early April, mark up a row 15cm from the edge for chard, New Zealand spinach, garlic and nasturtiums. Level with the cucumbers, plant clumps of garlic spaced 10cm apart, each consisting of five or six cloves. In mid-April, sow rainbow chard in every second gap between the garlic clumps. At the end of April, hoe the winter purslane (from Bed 7 on page 79).

Mid-May In the centre, plant and stake tomatoes spaced 1.2m apart, and sow a cucumber from seed between them, with the cucumbers going where the sweetcorn and beans will grow in the Native American bed (Bed 1 on page 66). Under the tomatoes, broadcast sow pot marigolds, which can then be thinned out a lot. Plant a New Zealand spinach plant and a nasturtium plant between the garlic clumps. Then mark up a planting spot 15cm away from the other edge, level with the tomatoes. Plant either one basil plant

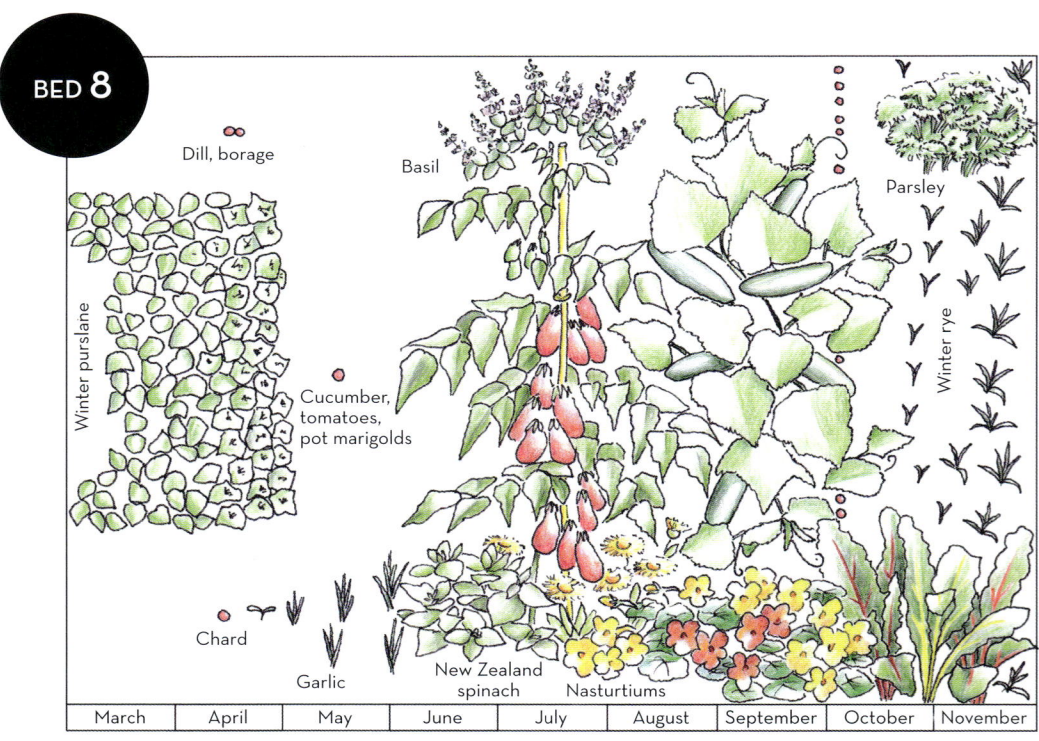

BED 8

or two parsley plants, or sow some dill or borage, at the planting spot.
Summer Regularly pinch out the tomatoes, tie them up and train the cucumber tendrils. If borage, pot marigolds, New Zealand spinach and nasturtiums get to experience the secateurs, they will reward you with fresh shoots. When the garlic turns brown, harvest it.
October If you wish, you can undersow winter rye (at a density of 300 seeds/m²) from September until the end of the first week in October. Then either hoe it out the following May and start again with the Native American bed (Bed 1), or allow it to grow. All vegetable patches benefit from having an occasional break when a cereal crop is grown instead.

GOOD PARTNERS

In scientific trials, tomatoes when grown outdoors together with cucumbers, garlic, basil and pot marigolds produced higher yields than when they were grown as a single crop. Garlic improved the quality of the tomatoes and, when grown with cucumbers, produced higher yields. Pot marigolds suppressed *Alternaria* fungi (moulds) in tomatoes. Parsley is said to improve the flavour of tomato fruits. The other plants keep the soil under the tomatoes covered, which greatly benefits the tomatoes.
Chard I love the variety mixes with colourful stalks such as 'Bright Lights' and 'Rainbow'. They look wonderful and grow really well. After harvesting, in the kitchen I separate the stalks from the leaves, and freeze the leaves for use in vegetable pies.
Parsley If you purchase young plants, growing them is child's play – just leave them to it and harvest a few leaves at a time. Curly-leaved parsley tastes better in salads, whereas flat-leaved parsley is better in stews.
Nasturtiums Not only do they repel aphids, but also the pungent-tasting leaves and flowers have an antibiotic effect on the bladder, kidneys and bronchi, repel *Candida* fungi (yeasts) and contain high levels of vitamin C. They should always be eaten fresh (40g daily is sufficient).
Winter rye This can still be sown as green manure in early October, as it is not killed off by frost, but continues to grow in spring and is ready for cutting in August. You can then sow lyme grass in August, which will succumb to the winter frosts. This gives the vegetable plot a year's rest, which greatly reduces the number of disease-causing pathogens in the soil.

Pot marigolds, basil, New Zealand spinach, garlic and nasturtiums under staked tomatoes.

NEW ZEALAND SPINACH

Not frost hardy, but robust and heat resistant if given sufficient water, this is a fantastic spinach substitute in the summer. The young leaves are also really tasty when eaten raw.

MIXED-ROW CULTIVATION FOR THE ADVENTUROUS

On this large template bed you will find 12 rows of vegetables spaced 50cm apart from each other, not counting the spinach rows. A row spacing of 40cm is sufficient for the vegetables, but a 50cm spacing is easier to work with.

Every year the rows move 25–30cm further on, so that the next year's rows of vegetables grow on the former spinach rows. It is a good idea to use fixed points such as fence posts, a bench, a tree or something similar when you are doing the annual measuring up. Here are a few general tips first, before you get to the instructions for the individual vegetable rows on the next pages.

The garden is calling The early bees are flying into the open crocuses, and it's T-shirt weather again at last! I rush out into my vegetable garden and mark up my spinach rows with small sticks every 50cm. Then I rake the mulch and harvest remnants to one side. When the ground is dry, the soil is warm enough and the forecast is for a longer period of warm weather, I make furrows in the soil and sow spinach or orache. Leaf lettuce is also suitable, especially where chard or beetroot is going to be planted next to it. For this I need a plan.

The plan I run through everything that I can sow in March. There is quite a lot, but I'm in no rush – there is still time in April, too. In any case, prolonged cold spells can slow down the March sowings, or even destroy them. At least I can start to spread compost for the heavy feeders, after first pulling the mulch to one side. Afterwards I either sow a green manure into the compost or pull the mulch back over it again. I also add compost to the planting holes when planting some of the heavy feeders.

Spinach rows I sow the spinach in March or early April. As soon as it starts to flower, I hoe it out and leave it lying. Now the spinach rows are my rows for walking, fertilising, mulching and watering. Over the summer they are always covered thickly with mulch so that plenty of humus can form underneath, because in the next year there will be vegetables in the spinach row. I mix into it coarse harvest remnants, grass cuttings from my neighbours and a lot of other food for the soil organisms. When watering, I do not water the vegetable rows directly. It is much better to water into the mulch so that the soil does not suffer as much. The spinach rows in the bed plan are partly replaced by leaf lettuce if the same plant family is due to grow next to it. Alternatively, leaf salad or broad beans can be sown, depending on the neighbouring planting.

Dividing up rows As we only need small amounts of some vegetables, I like to divide up the rows (e.g. 1m of rocket, 1m of radishes and 1m of autumn turnips). In the following plan you can substitute other vegetables for many of those specified, but always make sure that a particular plant family only occupies the same place once every four years (see page 43). This is also important in companion planting.

Autumn jobs If rows become empty early, I either sow another green manure or cover them with autumn leaves. With the digging fork I only loosen up the soil if the ground is very compacted. This becomes less necessary with each year that passes.

1. Carrots and leeks protect each other from pests. This works even better if they are planted close together in a single row.

2. In companion planting, lettuce protects kohl rabi from flea beetles.

COLOURFUL ROW PLAN

On nutrient-rich, loose, humus-rich garden soil a thick layer of surface compost is sufficient for the heavy feeders. However, if you have some available, you can add a layer of well-rotted compost in the spring.

Row 1: Cauliflower-celeriac-Florence fennel In mid-April, plant early cauliflower at 80cm intervals; early head cabbage and kohl rabi are also suitable. In mid-May, plant one celeriac in each of the gaps. When you harvest the cauliflowers around mid-July, replace each of them with a Florence fennel bulb. Harvest the celeriac and Florence fennel before the first hard frost.

Spinach

Row 2: Early lettuce-leek-summer purslane In early April, sow early varieties of iceberg, butterhead or loose-leaf lettuce at 30cm intervals, using a few seeds for each grouping. Later on, retain only the strongest plant, transfering other young plants to other rows. From mid-May, plant the winter leek variety 'Blaugrüner Winter' at 30cm intervals exactly halfway between the lettuces. When you have harvested the lettuces, earth up the leeks and broadcast sow summer purslane around them.

Spinach

Row 3: Cucumber-basil-lamb's lettuce In March, broadcast sow white mustard, which you can then hoe out in mid-May. When it has dried out somewhat after hoeing, pull it to the side, plant basil at 40cm intervals and sow in between them groups of three cucumber seeds. When the cucumbers gradually break down from August due to mildew, broadcast sow lamb's lettuce or phacelia for the winter harvest.

Leaf lettuce instead of spinach

Row 4: Beetroot-coriander-dill-chard At the end of April, sow rainbow chard in one part of the row, and beetroot, dill and coriander in the rest of the row, sowing only one seed of dill or coriander every 10cm. The leaves of dill and coriander will create some shade but they must not be allowed to overcrowd the beetroot. The latter can be thinned out a little after germination, but if you want baby beets (the size of golf balls) you need to allow them to grow fairly densely.

Leaf lettuce

Row 5: Beans-savory-lamb's lettuce In March, broadcast sow white mustard, which you can then hoe out in mid-May. From mid-May, sow dwarf beans such as 'Maxi' in clumps. After every fourth clump, leave an extra 15cm of space and there sow annual savory, marked by a small stick so that the tiny seedlings are not lost. Either cut the beans down after the first harvest and then sow two rows of lamb's lettuce for the autumn harvest, or wait for the second harvest and then after cutting down the beans sow lamb's lettuce for the spring harvest. In trials, beans grown together with lettuces produced higher yields, so lettuce is included alongside the beans in the plan.

Spinach

Row 6: Kohl rabi-lettuce-horseradish-radishes In mid-April, plant this row with early kohl rabi alternating with early butterhead lettuce and iceberg lettuce varieties at intervals of 25cm. If required, sow horseradish or radishes here and there between the lettuces instead of kohl rabi, or sow cress or rocket in between, in a double row if you prefer. Wherever you harvest, plant or sow something again in the gaps so that lettuces and small brassicas grow in colourful variety all year round. Often young plants are already growing before the plants next to them have been harvested. The lettuces protect the brassicas from cabbage flea beetles. In summer use bolt-resistant

MODEL BEDS FOR THE ADVENTUROUS

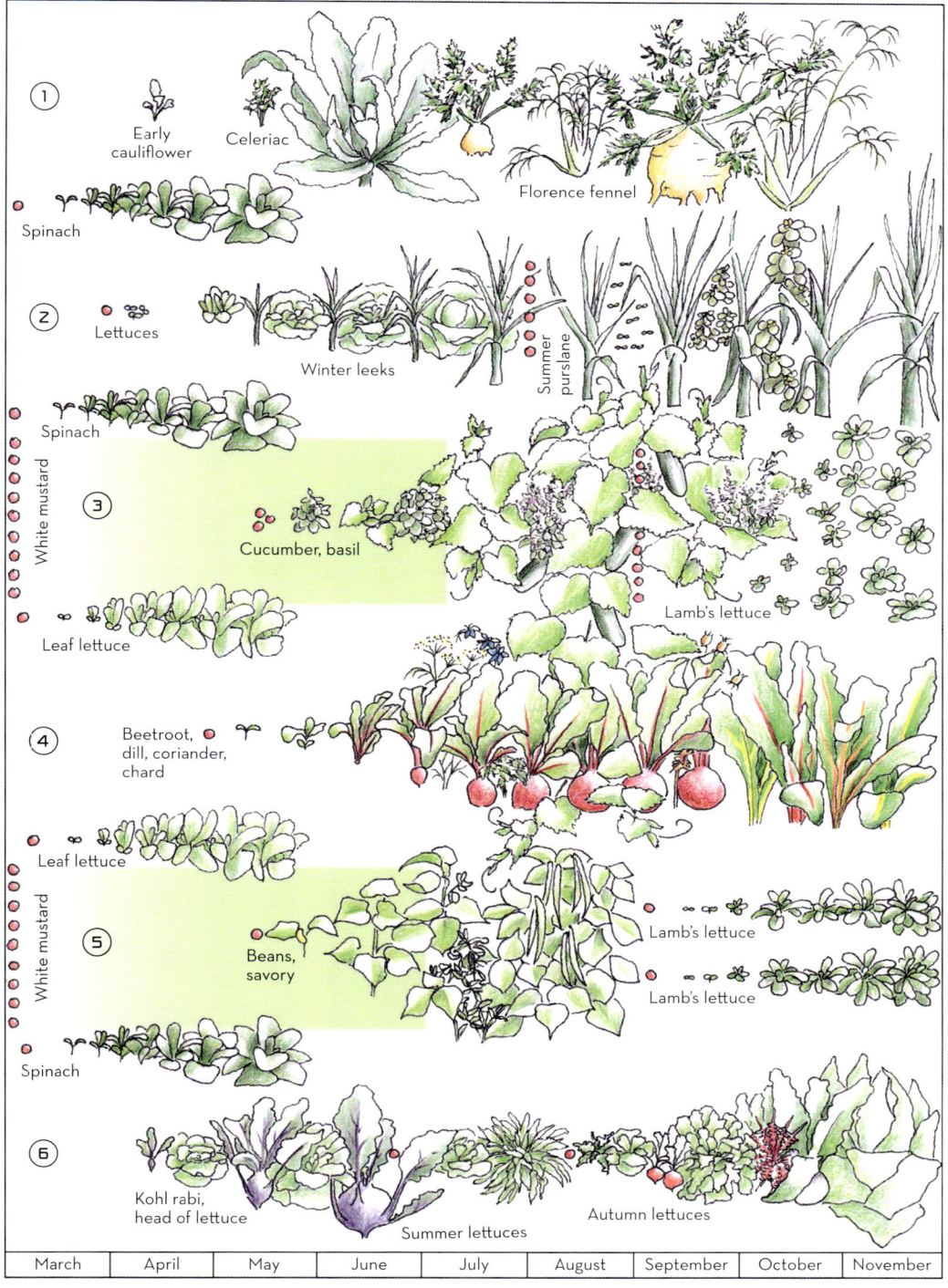

varieties; from August onward you can plant autumn lettuces such as winter endive, sugarloaf chicory, mizuna, Abyssinian cabbage, cima di rapa, pak choi, rocket or autumn turnips and Siberian kale in between. In trials when endive was grown together with rocket it produced increased yields.

Spinach

Row 7: Carrots–garlic–dill–black cumin–parsnips Divide the row into three sections. At the end of March, sow parsnips with some black cumin in one section. In mid-April, sow early carrots in the second section and place a garlic clove at 20cm intervals in between. Both rows will be ready to harvest at the same time in summer, after which this part of the row will become a double row of autumn spinach. Up to the end of April, in the third section of the row, sow carrots for storing (for example, 'Rothild'), together with some dill. Dill promotes the germination of carrot seeds, and should be harvested when it grows over the carrots. In mid-May, plant marjoram in any gaps here, to protect against carrot fly. Harvest the carrots for storing before the first hard frost; the parsnips can stay in the ground over winter. In trials, when carrots were grown together with lettuces they produced higher yields.

Spinach

Row 8: Shallots–onions–chamomile In March or April, divide the row and plant shallots in one half at 20cm intervals. In April, plant onion sets in the other half at 8cm intervals and sow a little chamomile in between. Harvest the onions and shallots when the onion foliage has almost completely died back. This will now leave room for the rampant growth of the courgettes and squashes from Row 9.

Spinach

Row 9: Sweetcorn–courgettes–squashes In March or April, sow a double row (spacing the rows 20cm apart) of turnips, leaf lettuce, radishes, horseradish and rocket to provide a colourful medley. In early May, free up space for the sweetcorn and then sow clumps each consisting of three kernels, with some spacing, at intervals of 1m. In mid-May, harvest and empty the planting plots for the courgettes and squashes, and each time plant one courgette plant between two sweetcorn clumps or one squash plant for every three sweetcorn plants. From September, sow winter purslane or lamb's lettuce over Rows 8, 9 and 10, so that it covers the ground between everything that is still standing.

Spinach

Row 10: Peas From early April, sow sugarsnap peas or marrowfat peas. Select a low to medium-height variety and support the plants with canes. Peas produced increased yields when grown together with rocket and lettuce in trials. After the peas have been harvested, the squashes and courgettes from Row 9 can grow rampantly.

Spinach

Row 11: Cabbage varieties–celery–herbs From March, sow white mustard, which you can hoe out in mid-May. From mid-May, plant brassicas such as late white cabbage, red cabbage, Savoy cabbage, broccoli, Brussels sprouts and kale, always at 60cm intervals. Here and there substitute two celery plants for one brassica, spacing them 30cm apart, which deters pests from brassicas. Sow herbs such as pot marigolds, French marigolds, borage, nasturtiums and chervil alongside the brassica row. They should not crowd the brassicas, but flower around them. French marigolds and pot marigolds suppress root nematodes. Borage and nasturtiums deter cabbage pests, slugs and snails, and chervil repels slugs, snails, ants and aphids. In trials, brassicas produced increased yields when grown in the vicinity of peas and lettuces.

Spinach

Row 12: Lettuces–black salsify–leaf chicory From April, divide the row into three sections and sow black salsify in the first section, loose-leaf lettuces in the second, and leaf chicory in the third. When the loose-leaf lettuces have been harvested, plant iceberg and batavia lettuces instead. From mid-August, winter endives and sugarloaf chicory can be planted.

MODEL BEDS FOR THE ADVENTUROUS

COMPANION PLANTING

HELPFUL PLANNING TIPS

Here you will find at a glance the plants described in this book together with their nutrient and space requirements, and the sowing, planting and harvesting times. Plant families are also listed, using the following abbreviations:

Am = amaranth family and goosefoot family,
Ai = Aizoaceae family, Bo = borage family,
Br = brassica family, Bu = buttercup family,
D = daisy family, La = labiate family, Le = legume family, M = mallow family, Na = nasturtium family,
Ni = nightshade family, O = onion family,
Pl = plantain family, Pu = purslane family,

R = rose family, Sa = sage family,
Sq = squash family, Sw = sweetgrass family,
U = umbellifer family, Va = valerian family,
Ve = verbena family.

Nutrient requirements are designated by the letter x (where x = very low and xxxx = very high).

Type of vegetable	Nutrient	Space requirement	Sowing times	Planting times	Harvesting
Abyssinian cabbages, Br	xx	2–5 × 25	April and Aug	–	May and Sept/Oct
Autumn turnips, Br	xx	10 × 30	July to mid-Aug	–	Sept to Nov
Basil, La	xx	25 × 30	–	From mid-May	June to mid-Oct
Beetroot (baby beets), Am	xx	4 × 12	Mid-April to mid-July	–	June to Sept
Beetroot, Am	xx	8 × 30	Mid-April to late June	–	July to Oct
Black cumin, Bu	x	1 × 20	March/April	–	Sept
Black salsify, D	xx	10 × 30	April	–	Oct to March
Borage, Bo	xxx	25 × 30	April to June	–	June to Oct
Broad beans, Le	x	15 × 50	Late Feb to April	–	June to Aug
Broccoli, Br	xxxx	50 × 50	–	Mid-April to late July	June to Nov
Brussel sprouts, Br	xxxx	50 × 60	–	May/June	Oct to March
Buck's horn plantain, Pl	x	15 × 15	April to Aug	–	All year round
Chamomile, As	x	3 × 15	April to May	–	June to Sept
Carrots (early), U	x	2–3 × 30	Mid-April to late June	–	July to Oct
Carrots (late), U	x	3–4 × 30	Mid-April to early May	–	Oct/Nov

HELPFUL PLANNING TIPS

Type of vegetable	Nutrient	Space requirement	Sowing times	Planting times	Harvesting
Cauliflower (autumn varieties), Br	xxxx	60 × 60	-	Mid-June to late July	Sept/ Oct
Cauliflower (early varieties), Br	xxxx	50 × 50	-	From mid-April	July
Cauliflower (summer varieties), Br	xxxx	60 × 60	-	May to June	July/Aug
Celeriac, U	xxx	40 × 40	-	Mid-May	mid-Oct
Celery, U	xxx	25 × 30	-	Mid-May to mid-July	Aug to Oct
Chard, A	xx	25 × 40	Mid-April to mid-July	-	June to Nov
Chervil, U	x	15 × 20	March to Sept	-	April to Nov
Chicory, D	x	10 × 40	Mid- to late May	-	Feb to April
Chinese cabbage, Br	xxxx	40 × 50	Mid-July	-	Sept to Nov
Chinese mallow, M	xx	25 × 25	March to Aug	-	Mid-June to Oct
Chives, O	x	20 × 30	-	April	April to Oct
Cima di rapa, Br	x	15 × 20	Mid-Aug	-	Sept/Oct
Coriander, U	x	12 × 25	April/May	-	End of July/Aug
Courgettes, Sq	xxx	80 × 120	-	Mid-May to late July	June to Oct
Cress, Br	x	1 × 10	March to Sept	-	April to Nov
Cucumber, Sq	xxx	30 × 120	Mid-May to mid-June	-	July to Sept
Daikon, Br	xxx	30 × 30	Late April to July	-	July to Oct
Dill, U	x	10 × 25	April to July	-	May to Oct
Dwarf beans, Le	x	8 × 40	Mid-May to mid-July	-	July to Sept
Florence fennel, U	xxx	30 × 30	-	From mid-May or late July/early Aug	From Aug or Oct
French marigolds (small), D	xxx	20 × 20	-	Mid-May	-
Garlic-chives, O	x	20 × 30	-	April	March to Nov
Garlic, O	xx	10 × 30	-	Mid-March to mid-April	Aug
Horseradish (early), Br	xx	10 × 25	April/May	-	June/July

Type of vegetable	Nutrient	Space requirement	Sowing times	Planting times	Harvesting
Horseradish (summer), Br	xx	20 × 25	May/June	–	June to Sept
Horseradish (winter), Br	xx	20 × 25	July to mid-Aug	–	Oct
Japanese greens, Br	xx	10 × 30	March/April and Aug/Sept	–	April/May and Sept to Dec
Kale, Br	xxx	50 × 50	–	May to mid-July	Sept to March
Kohl rabi (giant varieties), Br	xxx	40 × 40	–	May/June	Sept/Oct
Kohl rabi (normal-sized varieties), Br	xxx	25 × 30	–	Mid-April to mid-Aug	June to Nov
Lamb's lettuce, Va	x	7 × 15	March and late July to Sept	–	Sept to May
Leaf celery, U	xx	25 × 25	–	Mid-May	June to Dec
Leaf chicory, D	x	10 × 25	April to July	–	May to May
Leeks (autumn), O	xxx	20 × 30	–	April/May	Sept to Nov
Leeks (winter), O	xxx	20 × 30	–	May to July	Sept to April
Lettuces, D	xx	1 × 20 to 40 × 40	March to Sept	April to Aug	April to Nov
Marjoram, La	xx	20 × 20	–	Mid-May	June to Sept
May turnips, Br	xx	10 × 25	March/April and July/Aug	–	May/June and Sept/Oct
Nasturtiums, Na	xx	30 × 35 to 50 × 120	Mid-May	Mid-May	July to Oct
New Zealand spinach, Ai	xx	60 × 80	–	Mid-May	July to Oct
Onions (onion sets), O	xx	3-5 × 25	–	April	July/Aug
Orache, Am	xx	20 × 30	March to May	–	April to July
Pak choi, Br	xx	March, 2 × 10; July, 20 × 30	Late March and July to early Aug	–	Early May only baby leaves and Sept to Nov
Palm kale, Br	xxx	30 × 40	–	Mid-May	July to Oct
Parsley, U	x	20 × 30	–	April to July	June to Nov
Parsnips, U	x	15 × 30	March to mid-April	–	Oct to April
Pot marigolds, D	x	20 × 20	March to June	–	June to Oct
Potatoes, Ni	xxx	30 × 75	–	Mid-April to early May	July/Aug
Radishes, Br	x	3 × 15	April to Sept	–	May to Oct

Type of vegetable	Nutrient	Space requirement	Sowing times	Planting times	Harvesting
Red cabbage (early), Br	xxx	40 × 50	–	Mid-April	July
Red cabbage (late), Br	xxx	50 × 60	–	May/June	Sept to Nov
Rocket, Br	x	2 × 25	March to early Sept	–	April to Oct
Romanesco, Br	xxx	40 × 50	–	June/July	Aug to Oct
Root parsley, U	x	7 × 30	March/April	–	Oct to March
Runner beans, Le	xx	10 × 100	Mid-May to late June	–	July to Oct
Salsify, D	xx	10 × 30	April	–	Oct to Feb
Savory, La	x	25 × 25	Mid-May to late July	–	mid-July to late Oct
Savoy cabbage (storing variety), Br	xxx	50 × 50	–	April/May	Sept/Oct
Shallots, O	x	15 × 30	–	March/April	July/Aug
Siberian kale, Br	–	–	March/April and Sept	–	April to June and Oct to March
Spinach, Am	xxx	2-5 × 25	March to Sept	–	All year round
Squash, Sq	xxx	100 × 120 to 200 × 200	–	Mid-May	Mid-Oct
Strawberries, R	xxx	30 × 60	–	Aug	June/July
Sugarsnap peas, Le	x	4-5 × 30	April/May	–	June to Aug
Summer purslane, Pu	xx	15 × 20	Mid-May to mid-Aug	–	June to Oct
Swede, Br	x	40 × 50	May/June	July to early Aug	Aug to Nov
Sweetcorn, Sw	xxx	20 × 60	Mid-May	–	Aug/Sept
Tomatoes, Ni	xxx	60 × 70	–	Mid-May	July to mid-Oct
White cabbage (early), Br	xxx	40 × 40	–	Mid-April	June
White cabbage (late), Br	xxxx	50 × 60	–	May to mid-June	Sept/Oct
Winter purslane, Sa	x	1 × 15	Aug to Sept	–	Oct to April
Yacon, D	xxx	80 × 100	–	Mid-May	Oct

INDEX

Bold pagination refers to photographs;
italic pagination refers to planting layouts

A
advantages of companion planting 10
allelopathy 6, 9, 39
amaranth family 13, 43, 88–91
antibiotic 81
aphids 13
    plant repellents 26, 27, 36, 78, 81, 86
    predators 14, 37
autumn tasks 19, 44, 64, 82

B
basil 13, 88; **30, 81**
    container planting 52, 53, 55; *52, 53, 54, 55*
    increasing yields 28, 81
    outdoor variety 29
    sample beds 28, 29, 30, 34, 36, 46, 57, 67, 80, 81, 84; *29, 31, 35, 37, 47, 66, 80, 85*
bean aphids 26, 36, 78
beans 8, 12
    container planting 52, 54; *52, 54*
    increasing yields 8, 50, 67, 78, 84
    pests 15, 26, 36, 78
beans, broad 82, 88
    sample beds 36, 37, 50, 57, 70; *37, 51, 71*
beans, field 67; **73**
    green manure 62, 63, 65
    sample beds 50, 57, 62, 72–73; *51, 72*
beans, French (dwarf) 13, 67, 89
    sample beds 26, 27, 46, 48, 54, 78, 84; *27, 47, 49, 54, 79, 85*
beans, runner 27, 37, 67, 91; **15**
    container planting 52; *52*
    sample beds 34–35, 66, 67
    scarlet 14, 52, 67
beet cyst eelworm 62
beet leaf miner 43
beet, fodder 79
beetroot 13, 43, 82, 88
    container planting 53, 55; *53, 55*
    increasing yields 46, 78
    pests 15, 62
    sample beds 30–31, 46, 70, 78, 79, 84; *31, 47, 71, 79, 85; 30, 79*
beetroot, baby beets 31, 88; **79**
    sample beds 53, 55, 78, 84; *53, 79*
beginners
    mixed row cultivation 44–51
    mulch ABC 17
    tips 22–23
biochemical reaction 6, 8, 9
blight
    potato 43, 73
    tomato 28, 29, 43, 56
borage 42, 88–91; **71**
sample beds 55, 70, 71, 81, 86; *55, 71, 80*
brassica family 43, 86, 88–91
broccoli 88; **25**
    increasing yields 50
    regrowing 25
    sample beds 24, 25, 50, 54, 86; *24, 51, 54*
brussels sprouts 26, 27, 86, 88; *27, 29*
buckwheat 42, 63
butterfly, cabbage white 25, 28, 43, 50

C
cabbage 23, 43
    sample beds 28, 48, 76, 84, 86; *29, 49, 77*
cabbage, Abyssinian 47, 48, 88
    sample beds 30, 31, 55, 86; *31*
cabbage, Chinese 61, 89
    sample beds 53, 68, 69; *53, 69*
cabbage pests
    butterfly 25, 28, 43, 50
    fly 43, 68, 76
    flea beetle 43, 46, 47, 68, 78, 84
cabbage, pointed 28
cabbage, red 28, 76, 86, 91; *77*
cabbage, Savoy 28, 86, 91
cabbage, white 28, 86, 91
carrot 13, 23, 88
    increasing yields 48, 68, 74, 86
    pest repellent 74, 83
    sample beds 32–33, 48, 55, 56, 68, 74, 86; *32, 49, 55, 69, 75, 87*
    storage variety 33
carrot pests 15
    fly 33, 43, 48, 69, 73, 74, 76, 83, 86
caterpillars, moth 25, 43
cauliflower 14, 89, 65; **77**
    increasing yields 50
    sample beds 50, 54, 76, 84; *54, 85*
    romanesco 76, 91
celeriac 15, 23, 65, 89, 90; **25**
    increasing yields 25
    sample beds 24–25, 50, 76, 84; *24, 51, 77, 85*
celeriac rust 25, 50
celery 50, 78, 89
    sample beds 54, 76–77, 86; *54, 77, 87*
chamomile 88
    sample beds 38, 54, 57, 86; *38, 54, 87*
chard 26, 82, 89
    increasing yields 46
    pests 62
    sample beds 55, 80, 81, 84; *54, 80, 85*
chard, Swiss 43, 46; *47*
chervil 43, 55, 69, 89
    pest repellent 38, 68, 86
chicory 61, 89
    sample beds 74, 75; *75*
chicory, leaf 61, 90; **75**
    container planting 52; *52*
    sample beds 55, 74, 75, 86; *75, 87*
chicory, sugarloaf 61
    sample beds 46, 48, 55, 86; *55*
chives 13, 39, 43, 57, 89
container planting 53, 57; *53*
cima di rapa 86, 89
clover
    green manure 63
    paths 44–46, 48, 50; *47, 49, 51;* **45**
clover varieties
    crimson 46, 48, 63; *49;* **63**
    Egyptian 63
    Persian 63
    white 44, 57, 76; **45**
clubroot 43, 62
colourful beds 80–81, 84, 86; *80, 85, 87*
compost basics 16, 23, 52
container planting, small 52–53
coriander 43, 89
    sample beds 36, 38, 46, 55, 84; *37, 38, 47, 55, 85*
couch grass 65
courgette 13, 23, 89; **34**
    increasing yields 34, 46, 67
    sample beds 34–35, 46, 47, 54–55, 67, 86; *35, 54, 66, 87*
cress 33, 43, 84, 89; *32*
crop rotation 33, 42, 62, 77, 82
    four-year 54–55
    ten-year 22
cucumber 12, 13, 89
    container planting 52, 55; *52, 55*
    increasing yields 31, 46, 57, 67, 81
    sample beds 30–31, 46, 57, 66, 67, 80–81, 84; *31, 47, 80, 85*
cumin, black 74, 75, 86, 88; *75, 87*

D
dill 13, 43, 89
    container planting 52, 53, 54, 55; *52, 53, 54, 55*
    sample beds 32–33, 36, 46, 48, 74, 80, 81, 84, 86; *32, 37, 47, 49, 75, 80, 85, 87*

E
eelworm, beet cyst 62
endive 13, 31, 60, 61; **60**
    sample beds 48, 36, 55; *37, 55*
endive, winter 61
    sample beds 30, 36, 46, 78, 79, 86; *31, 79*
eucalyptus 17

F
families 43, 88–91
fennel 43
fennel, Florence 30, 89
    sample beds 68, 76, 77, 84; *69, 77, 85*
fertiliser 16; *see also* green manure; soil condition
flea beetle
    cabbage stem 43, 46, 47, 68, 78, 83, 84
    striped 26, 27
fly, cabbage root 43, 68
Franck, Gertrud 9

G
garlic 38, 43, 89; **30**

INDEX

increasing yields 28, 39, 50, 69, 81
    sample beds 28, 39, 40, 41, 50, 55, 57, 68, 69, 80–81, 86; *29, 38, 40, 51, 55, 69, 80, 87*
    see also rocambole
garlic chives 39, 43, 89
    sample beds 40, 41, 53; *40, 53*
gooseberry, cape 13; **13**
goosefoot, giant (tree spinach) 43, 70–71; *71*
green manure 19, 23, 62–63
    bed preparation 66
    pest control 15
    soil compaction 65
    sowing 18, 36–37, 42, 44, 50, 56, 62–63, 81, 82
    see also horsetail tea; nettle slurry; soil condition; tansy powder
ground elder 65

H

harvest times 88–91
    salad vegetables 61
hedge trimmings 39
herb window box 53
hoeing 18
holly 17
horseradish 43, 89–90
    sample beds 46–48, 68, 84, 86
horsetail 65
    tea 72–73
humus 10, 16, 82

I

increasing yields 6, 10, 14
    basil 28, 81
    beans 8, 50, 67, 78, 84
    beetroot 46, 78
    brassicas 86
    broccoli 50
    carrot 48, 68, 74, 86
    cauliflower 50
    celeriac 25
    chard 46
    courgette 34, 46, 67
    cucumber 31, 46, 57, 67, 81
    garlic 28, 39, 50, 69, 81
    kohl rabi 78
    leek 25, 48
    lettuce 28, 46, 68, 69, 74, 84, 86
    onion 31, 39
    peas 67, 68, 69, 86
    pot marigold 28, 81
    potato 50
    squash 67
    strawberries 39
    sweetcorn 8, 34, 50, 67
    tomato 28, 57, 81
indicator plants, soil
    compaction 65
    nutrient-rich 11, 16, 64
insects, beneficial 14
intercropping 8
irrigation *see* watering

J

Japanese greens 90; **26**
    mizuna 27, 86
    sample beds 26–27, 46, 47, 48; *27*

K

kale 90
    sample beds 26, 27, 68, 70; *27, 69*
kale, palm, sample beds 27, 76; *77;* **7, 76**
kale, Siberian,: sample beds 76, 77, 78, 86; *77, 79*
kohl rabi 13, 34, 90; **78, 83**
    container planting 52
    increasing yields 78
    sample beds 26, 46, 47, 55, 70, 78, 84; *27, 47, 54, 55, 71, 79, 85*
kohl rabi, giant 78, 90; *79*

L

Langerhorst, Jakobus & Margarete 9
Langerhorst, Margarete, potato bed 72–73
leek 23, 90; **25, 77, 83**
    increasing yields 25, 48
    mould/pest repellent 25, 39, 48, 76
    pests and diseases 25, 43, 48
    sample beds 24, 25, 48, 76, 84; *24, 49, 77, 85;* **25, 77, 83**
legume family 12, 43, 67, 88–91; **12**
lettuce 60–61, 68; **60, 70, 78, 83**
    container planting 52, 53, 54, 55; *54, 55*
    increasing yields 28, 46, 68, 74, 84, 86
    pest repellent 26, 46, 78, 83, 84
    pests 15
    roots/nutrient levels 11, 12, 13, 17, 90
    sowing/harvesting 60–61, 90
    wheat suppression 7
    winter varieties 60, 61, 74, 76; *75, 77*
lettuce, Batavia 48, 61, 86
lettuce, butterhead 13, 60, 61
    container planting 53, 55; *53*
    sample beds 28, 84; *29*
lettuce, cos 13, 46, 48, 61; **60**
    container planting 55
lettuce, iceberg 13, 48, 60, 61, 84, 86
    container planting 55
lettuce, lamb's 13, 60, 61, 90
    container planting 53, 54, 55; *54, 55*
    sample beds 26, 28, 30, 36–37, 38, 46, 48, 50, 57, 84, 86; *27, 29, 37, 38, 47, 51, 85, 87*
lettuce, leaf 61, 82
    container planting 52, 53, 54, 55; *54*
    sample beds 26, 27, 46, 48, 57, 68, 70, 71, 84, 86; *27, 85, 87*
lettuce, loose-leaf 13, 61
    container planting 54; *54*
    sample beds 26, 30, 46, 48, 68, 70, 71, 78, 84, 86; *27, 31, 79, 87*
lettuce, oakleaf 61
lettuce, rocket 13, 43, 50, 61, 70, 91
    container planting 53, 55; *55*
    sample beds 30, 31, 46, 47, 48, 57, 68, 69, 84, 86; *31, 69*
light conditions, optimum 14

lupin 65
lyme grass 42, 40, 62, 63, 65, 81; **63**

M

mallow, Chinese 13, 61, 89
    green manure 42, 65
    sample beds 33, 50, 55, 68, 69; *32, 51, 55, 69*
marigold, French 89; **15, 29**
    nematodes 15, 39
    sample beds 28, 38, 55, 86; *29, 38, 55*
marigold, pot 81, 90; **81**
    container planting 53; *53*
    increasing yields 28, 81
    sample beds 28, 29, 38, 50, 54, 56, 80, 81, 86; *29, 38, 51, 54, 80*
marjoram 55, 86, 90; *55*
marking beds 22–23, 44
    marker sowing 43, 58
mildew (powdery) 30, 34, 35, 84
mixed row cultivation
    adventurous 82–87
    starter 44–51
monoculture 9
mould fungi 81
mould, grey 39, 41; **39**
mugwort 28
mulch basics
    compaction 65
    grass clippings 17, 26
    mini mulch ABC 17
    practical tips 6, 10, 14, 16–17, 18, 19, 54
    straw 38, 40, 41, 65
mulch for plants
    carrot-pea 32
    celeriac-leek-broccoli 24, 25
    clover path bed preparation 44, 46
    courgette-sweetcorn 34
    cucumber-beetroot-onion 30, 31
    lettuce-beans-brassica 26
    potato 50, 72, 73
    potato-bean-strawberry 36
    shallot-carrot-salsify-chicory 74
    spinach 82
    strawberry-garlic 38, 39, 40, 41, 42
    tomato-cabbage 28, 54
    yacon 70
mustard 15, 43
    sample beds 32, 36, 57; *37*
mustard, white
    and clubroot 62
    container planting 54, 55
    green manure 15, 44, 62, 63
    sample beds 34, 41, 46, 48, 70, 72, 73, 84, 86; *35, 40, 47, 49, 71, 72, 85, 87*

N

nasturtium 90; **7, 81**
    container planting 52, 53, 54; *52, 53, 54*
    sample beds 80, 81, 86; *80*
Native American planting 8, 66–67
nematodes 15, 29, 39, 62, 86
    potato cyst 43

pratylenchus 62
nettle slurry 23, 24–25, 28, 30
nettles as soil indicator 11, 16, 64
niger manure 63
nightshade family 43
nitrogen levels 12, 13–14
    grass cuttings 17
    legumes 12, 33, 36, 43, 50, 62, 69, 73
    white clover 44, 57
nutrients see soil condition

O

onion 90
    family 39, 40, 43, 88–91
    increasing yields 31, 39
    manure 73
    mulch 17, 39
    pests 15, 43
    sample beds 30–31, 38, 39, 48, 55, 86; *31, 38, 49, 55, 87*
onion fly 43, 48, 74
orache 13, 43, 82, 90; **71**
    sample beds 55, 57, 70–71; *55, 71*

P

pak choi 13, 43, 68, 86, 90; *69*
parsley 13, 43, 90
    sample beds/containers 28, 53, 54, 56, 81; *29, 53, 54, 80*
    see also root parsley
parsnip 43, 90
    sample beds 76, 77, 78, 86; *77, 87*
peas 43; **9**
    increasing yields 67, 68, 69, 86
    nitrogen mitigation 33, 50
    nutrient levels 12, 13
    pests 15
    sample beds 55, 86; *55, 86*
peas, sugarsnap 13, 91
    sample beds 32–33, 50, 68, 86; *32, 69; 33*
phacelia 15, 65; **12, 36**
    green manure 42, 50, 62, 63, 73
    sample beds 36, 46, 50, 55, 57, 67, 73, 84; *37, 47, 55, 66, 72*
plant families 43, 88–91
plantain
    broadleaf 65
    buck's horn 61, 68, 88; **68**
planting and sowing 18
    times 88–91
potato 13, 65, 90
    effect on tomatoes 29
    horsetail tea 72, 73
    increasing yields 50
    pests and diseases 15, 36, 43, 73
    sample beds 36, 50, 72–73; *37, 51, 72*
purslane 13, 88–91
purslane, summer 61
    sample beds 34, 35, 55, 84; *35, 55, 85*
purslane, winter 60
    container planting 52, 53
    sample beds 26, 33, 34, 50, 54, 55, 78, 80, 86; *27, 29, 32, 35, 54, 79, 80, 87*

R

radicchio 60, 61; **60,** *79*
    sample beds 46, 78; *79*
radish 11, 43, 82; **33**
    container planting 53
    nutrient levels 13, 90
    sample beds 26, 32, 33, 46–48, 54, 55, 68, 69, 76, 84, 86; *27, 32, 49, 54, 55, 69, 87*
radish varieties
    daikon 68, 69, 90; **69**
    oil 63, 65
    winter 68, 69
raised beds 54–55
rocambole 38, 39, 50; **39**; *see also* garlic
romanesco 76, 91
root depth
    deep 11, 12, 15, 60, 62, 76
    shallow 11, 12, 15, 76
root exudates (juglone and saponin) 9, 14, 44
root parsley 76, 77, 91; *77*
rye, winter 80, 81; *80*

S

salad vegetables, year-round 60–61, 75
salsify 76, 91; **74**
    pests 15, 74
    sample beds 74; *75*
salsify, black 76, 88; **74**
    sample beds 74, 86; *75, 87*
savory 91; **27**
    container planting 52, 54; *52, 54*
    sample beds 26, 27, 46, 78, 84; *27, 47, 79, 85*
seasonal jobs
    autumn 19, 44, 64, 82
    spring 18, 64
shallots 43, 48, 91
    sample beds 54, 74–75, 86; *54, 75, 87*
shield fern powder 33
snails and slugs 43
    fence 23; **23**
    repellent plants 38, 57, 67, 68, 86
soil condition 6, 10–13, 15, 16, 17, 19, 44, 56
    compaction 10, 11, 65, 82
    fatigue 9
    feeding 16, 18, 23, 24, 46, 52, 82, 84
    indicator plants 11, 16, 64, 65
    nutrient levels 10–13, 88–91
    reciprocal balancing 12, 14, 50
    see also green manure
sowing times 88–91
    salad vegetables 61
space requirements, plants 88–91
spinach 14, 43, 60, 61, 91; **15**
    container planting 52, 54, 55; *54, 55*
    New Zealand 80–81, 90; *80*
    nutrients 13
    pests 15
    sample beds 26, 30, 33, 34, 35, 44, 46–47, 48, 57, 76, 78, 82, 86; *27, 31, 35, 47, 49, 51, 77, 79, 85, 87*
    see also tree spinach

spring tasks 18, 64
squash 91; **67**
    increasing yields 67
    sample beds 66–67, 86; *66, 87*
straw (mulch/protection) 38, 40, 41, 65
strawberry 8, 91
    container planting 53; *53*
    increasing yields 39
    pests and diseases 15, 39, 41; **41**
    sample beds 36, 38, 39, 40, 42; *37, 38, 40, 42*
summer harvest tubs 52–53; *52–53*
sweetcorn 67, 91; **9, 34, 67**
    increasing yields 8, 34, 50, 67
    pests 15
    sample beds 34–35, 50, 66–67, 86; *35, 50, 66, 87*
sycamore 17

T

tansy 73; **73**
tansy powder 33, 48, 68, 73
'Three Sisters' planting 8; **8**
thuja 39
tomato 43, 91
    blight 28, 29, 43, 56
    container planting 53, 54; *53, 54*
    increasing yields 28, 57, 81
    nutrient levels 11, 13, 57, 62
    pest repellent 28
    pests and diseases 28, 29, 56, 81
    sample beds 28–29, 56–57, 80–81; *29, 80*
    suppression 9
toxicity, plant (allelopathy) 9
tree spinach (giant goosefoot) 43, 70–71; *71*
turnip 13, 43, 88, 90
    sample beds 55, 68; *55*
turnip, autumn
    sample beds 46, 47, 48, 78, 79, 86; *79*

U

umbelliferae 33, 43, 88–91

V

vetch, common 43, 63
voles 76

W

walnut, black 9, 17
watering 11, 16
weed suppression 16, 23, 62
    cardboard 64, 65
weeds and mulch making 17
wheat 7
whitefly 30, 43, 76
    cabbage 43, 68, 76

Y

yacon 15, 73, 91; **14, 70**
    sample beds 70–71; *71*
yew 39

PHOTO CREDITS

Key: Flora Press = FP, MI = Mauritius Images, SS = Shutterstock, BP = BIOSPHOTO, GAP = GAP Photos, AS = stock.adobe.com
T = Top, B = Bottom, C = Centre, R = Right, L = Left

FP/Ute Klaphake: 2. FP/Buiten-Beeld: 3T. FP/Daniela Kunze: 3BL, 31, 33R, 68. FP/Otmar Diez: 3BR, 20. GAP/ Friedrich Strauß Gartenbildagentur: 4. FP/Alexandre Petzold: 7T, 12C, 29, 41T. FP/Derek St. Romaine: 7B. MI/Alamy, Maggie Sully: 8. MI/Alamy, Michiel Vaarties: 9. SS/lllonajalll: 10. Otrud Grieb: 11, 13BR, 13TR, 15R, 17T, 17L, 17R, 18TL, 18TC, 18TR, 18BL, 18BR, 19TL, 19TR, 19B, 23, 25R, 27, 30, 34, 36, 39R, 45T, 45B, 60L, 60R, 63L, 63R, 67T, 70, 73R, 75, 77, 78, 81. SS/images72: 12L. SS/tamu1500: 14L. AS/ Jenny: 15L. SS/Artazum: 25L. SS/ElenVik: 26. SS/johan kusuma: 28. FP/FocusOnGarden/Sibylle Pietrek: 33L, 62.

FP/Meyer-Rebentisch: 37, 76. FP/Derek Harris: 39L. FP/Helga Noack: 41L FP/Flora Press: 41R. BP/Serge Lapouge: 64. GAP/Thomas Alamy: 65L, 65R. FP/GWI: 67B. SS/traction: 69. SS/Groeventhal: 71R. AS/orestligetka: 71C. SS/Heike Rau: 71B. FP/Ulrike Schmidt: 73L. FP/Christine Ann Föll: 74T. FP/Digitalice Images: 74B FP/Martin Hughes-Jones: 79L. SS/RaspberryStudio: 79R. FP/Evi Pelzer: 83 B. BP/NouN: 83T

All illustrations by Ortrud Grieb except AS/annarepp: 14R.

G/Images Professionals GmbH: front cover. GAP/Nicola Stocken, Marston and Langinger: back cover. Almuth Grieb: back cover flap. SS/Johan Kusama: inside cover, top. FP/Alexandre Petzold: inside cover, bottom.

GREEN BOOKS
Bloomsbury Publishing Plc
50 Bedford Square, London, WC1B 3DP, UK
Bloomsbury Publishing Ireland Limited,
29 Earlsfort Terrace, Dublin 2, D02 AY28, Ireland

BLOOMSBURY, GREEN BOOKS and the Green Books logo are trademarks of
Bloomsbury Publishing Plc

First published in 2022 in Germany as *Wer kann mit wem in Beet?* by Franckh-Kosmos Verlags-GmbH & Co. KG
First published in 2026 in the United Kingdom as *Companion Planting* by Bloomsbury Publishing Plc
This edition published by arrangement with Franckh-Kosmos Verlags-GmbH & Co. KG, Stuttgart, Germany

Copyright © Ortrud Grieb, 2022
Translation © Maureen Millington-Brodie, 2025

Ortrud Grieb has asserted her right under the Copyright, Designs and Patents Act, 1988, to be identified as Author of this work

All rights reserved. No part of this publication may be: i) reproduced or transmitted in any form, electronic or mechanical, including photocopying, recording or by means of any information storage or retrieval system without prior permission in writing from the publishers; or ii) used or reproduced in any way for the training, development or operation of artificial intelligence (AI) technologies, including generative AI technologies. The rights holders expressly reserve this publication from the text and data mining exception as per Article 4(3) of the Digital Single Market Directive (EU) 2019/790

Bloomsbury Publishing Plc does not have any control over, or responsibility for, any third-party websites referred to or in this book. All internet addresses given in this book were correct at the time of going to press. The author and publisher regret any inconvenience caused if addresses have changed or sites have ceased to exist, but can accept no responsibility for any such changes

A catalogue record for this book is available from the British Library
Library of Congress Cataloguing-in-Publication data has been applied for

ISBN: PB: 978-1-3994-2748-7; ePub: 978-1-3994-2749-4; ePDF: 978-1-3994-2746-3

2 4 6 8 10 9 7 5 3 1

Layout for this edition by Roderick Teasdale
Printed by Westermann Druck GmbH, Zwickau in Germany

To find out more about our authors and books visit www.bloomsbury.com and sign up for our newsletters
For product safety related questions contact productsafety@bloomsbury.com

Good neighbours — bad neighbours

PLANTS	GOOD NEIGHBOURS	BAD NEIGHBOURS
Basil	Courgettes, Cucumber, Florence Fennel, Tomato	—
Beetroot	Beans, Cabbages, Coriander, Courgette, Cucumber, Dill, Garlic, Kohl Rabi, Lettuces, Onion, Parsnips, Rocket, Savory	Carrots, Chard, Leeks, Potatoes, Spinach, Sweetcorn
Black Salsify	Carrots, Horseradish, Kohl Rabi, Leeks, Lettuces, Onion, Radishes	—
Borage	Beans, Cabbages, Cucumber, Lettuces, Peas, Potatoes, Tomato	—
Broad Beans	Basil, Cabbages, Carrots, Chervil, Lettuces, Orache, Phacelia, Potatoes, Savory, Spinach, Winter Purslane	Alliums, Beans, Peas
Cabbages	Bean, Beetroot, Borage, Carrot, Celeriac, Coriander, Cucumber, Dill, Endive, French Marigold, Leek, Lettuces, Parsnips, Peas, Pepper, Potatoes, Pot Marigold, Radishes, Spinach, Tomato	Chinese Cabbages, Garlic, Onion, Strawberries
Carrots	Black Salsify, Cabbages, Chard, Chicory, Chives, Coriander, Cress, Dill, Endive, French Marigold, Garlic, Horseradish, Leeks, Lettuces, Marjoram, Onion, Peas, Pepper, Pot Marigold, Radishes, Rocket, Rutabagas, Shallots, Spinach, Summer Purslane, Tomato	Beetroot, Parsley, Parsnips
Cauliflower, Broccoli	Broad Beans, Celeriac, Clover, Dill, Dwarf French Beans, Fennel, Lettuces, Peas, Phacelia, Pot Marigolds, Tomato	Cabbage
Celeriac	Beans, Cabbages, Chamomile, Cucumber, Kohl Rabi, Leeks, Spinach, Squash, Tomato	Carrots, Dill, Parsnips, Potatoes, Sweetcorn
Celery	Cabbages, Horseradish	Celeriac
Chamomile	Beans, Cabbages, Celeriac, Courgette, Lettuces, Onions, Peas, Potatoes, Spinach, Tomato	—
Chard	Basil, Beans, Cabbages, Carrots, Celeriac, Horseradish, Kohl Rabi, Lettuces, Onion, Parsnips, Radishes, Turnip	Beetroot, Black Salsify, Orache, Spinach
Chervil	Cabbages, Cucumber, Endive, Kohl Rabi, Lettuces	Radishes
Chicory, Radicchio	Beans, Beetroot, Carrots, Florence Fennel, Lettuces, Onion, Parsnips, Tomato	—
Chinese Cabbage	Beans, Carrots, Kohl Rabi, Lettuces, Orache, Peas, Spinach	Cabbages, Chard, Horseradish, Leek, Potatoes, Radishes
Chinese Mallow	Herbs, Potatoes	—
Chives	Carrots, Cucumber, Parsley, Tomato	Beans, Peas
Coriander	Cabbages, Cucumber, Horseradish, Potatoes, Spinach, Tomato	—
Courgette	Basil, Beans, Beetroot, Chamomile, Fennel, Lettuces, Nasturtium, Onion, Peas, Sweetcorn	Cucumber, Potatoes, Radishes